GOODBYE TO BOLEYN

GOODBYE TO BOLEYN

WEST HAM'S FINAL SEASON AT UPTON PARK AND THE BIG KICK-OFF AT STRATFORD

PETE MAY

Biteback Publishing

First published in Great Britain in 2016 by
Biteback Publishing Ltd
Westminster Tower
3 Albert Embankment
London SE1 7SP

ISBN 978-1-78590-147-8

10 9 8 7 6 5 4 3 2 1

A CIP catalogue record for this book is available from the British Library.

Set in Minion by Adrian McLaughlin
Icons made by Freepik from www.flaticon.com

Printed and bound in Great Britain by
CPI Group (UK) Ltd, Croydon CR0 4YY

CONTENTS

	Acknowledgements	*vii*
	Preface	*ix*
1	My West Ham family	1
2	Is that all we bring at home?	7
3	Goodbye to Boleyn	41
4	We've got Payet!	55
5	In Ken's Café we trust	81
6	Stick your blue flag up your…	89
7	A Christmas Carroll	109
8	My dad's last game	127
9	*Je t'aime, Dimitri*	137
10	Come on you Ironworks	159
11	Tottenham Hotspur – it's happened again!	169
12	More bookings at the Newham Bookshop	191

13 Drawing drawing West Ham 197
14 Win or lose we're on the booze 217
15 Concentrating on the Europa League 229
16 The final farewell 251
17 We're all going on a European tour 261
18 Olympian Hammers 271
19 London calling 293

ACKNOWLEDGEMENTS

FIRSTLY, THANKS TO ALL READERS OF MY HAMMERS IN the Heart blog, where I recorded some of the early versions of these chapters. I'm also indebted to my regular match-day companions, Matt George, Fraser Massey, Michael McManus and Nigel Morris, and also Ken's Café regulars Lisa Pritchard, Gavin Hadland, Carolyn Quinn, Denis Campbell, Joe Norris and Phill Jupitus. Thanks also go to numerous other Irons fans, including Alison O'Brien, Scott O'Brien, Steve Flory, Brian Williams, Steve Rapport, Shane Barber and the late Paul Garrett, who is now having a chat upstairs with Bobby Moore.

Thanks to the inimitable Carol and Ken Lucas and all at Ken's Café, Vivian Archer, John Newman and all at the Newham Bookshop, to the Black Lion for stocking real ale, to all the local traders at Upton Park and, of course, to Mr Moon. I'm also indebted to Steve Chamberlain for publishing my pieces on my West Ham family and my dad's last game in *The Guardian* (extended versions of which can be found in Chapters 1 and 8), to Iain Dale and all at Biteback for commissioning this book and to Victoria Godden for copy-editing. And finally, thanks to my wife Nicola and daughters Lola and Nell for putting up with my claret-and-blue obsessions.

Pete May blogs on West Ham at hammersintheheart.blogspot.co.uk

PREFACE

THIS ISN'T A BOOK ABOUT THE ECONOMICS OF STADIUM moves. Instead, what it hopefully captures is a sense of what it was like to be a fan at the Boleyn Ground for that final season and also at the first games at the sparkling new Olympic Stadium. Some chapters look back at my memories of attending games since the 1970s, while in the diary sections on 2015–16 I've tried to acknowledge the seasonal rhythms of the football fan, the minutiae of football trivia, the banter, the lucky shirts, the cafés and pubs, the chants, and the unforgettable atmosphere of the final home game against Manchester United.

For West Ham fans, the Boleyn Ground was the only home they had ever known. When West Ham first bid in 2012 to move from the Boleyn to the Olympic Stadium in Stratford, it all seemed aeons away. The fans continued to visit Ken's

Café, the Boleyn pub, the Central, the Ercan chip shop and myriad other pre- and post-match institutions.

Suddenly, however, it was the final season at the Boleyn, and the thirteen months from July 2015 to August 2016 saw massive changes as the Hammers swapped the tight, working-class streets of E13 for the shopping centre of Westfield and the concrete expanses of the Queen Elizabeth Olympic Park.

The club moved from the Memorial Grounds to the Boleyn Ground in 1904, the stadium taking its name from Green Street House, known as the Boleyn Castle because of its associations with Anne Boleyn, an early WAG of Henry VIII (a relationship that, like many a West Ham game, didn't end happily).

The ground became a central part of its community. Moore, Hurst and Peters had won the World Cup for England while at the Boleyn. Parades past the Boleyn pub marked the FA Cup wins of 1964, 1975 and 1980 and the European Cup Winners' Cup win of 1965.

Most West Ham fans could see the commercial logic of moving to a bigger home, but for the traditionalists there was also the fear that in the cash-dominated era of the Premier League another link to the roots of football was being lost. Pubs, cafés and stalls would go out of business and we'd no longer be close enough to the pitch for the players to hear our expletives. Would the new stadium ever be able to replicate the intimidating but intimate atmosphere of Upton Park? Football fans are by nature conservative, attached to routines. Relegation we can cope with; change is a little harder.

It would have been difficult for any owners to have turned down the Olympic Stadium, despite the fact that it was designed for athletics and not football. By the time the new roof had been built and retractable seating installed it had cost an estimated £701 million. West Ham would end up getting it for around £15 million, plus a £40 million loan from Newham Council – and as a bonus greatly annoy Spurs, who had made a controversial late bid to move to Stratford.

Owners David Gold and David Sullivan had bought a club with massive debts in 2010 but now saw not just a bargain but an opportunity to rise to the fabled 'next level'. West Ham could nearly double its capacity, from 35,000 to 60,000. With all that extra income, world-class players would be attracted. The new stadium was also much more accessible, having many more train and tube links than Upton Park, which is isolated on the District Line, and was still in the borough of Newham, just a couple of miles from the Boleyn.

Karren Brady, West Ham's vice-chairman, negotiated hard, knowing the London Legacy Development Corporation were desperate not to be left with a rusting 'white elephant' of a stadium. The club would have a 100-year lease and the rent would be a reasonable £2.5 million a year (and it's halved if West Ham are relegated, which as an Irons fan you always have to consider a possibility). And we get free goalposts and corner flags.

Yet, for all the apparent benefits, leaving home still hurts. West Ham played at the Boleyn Ground for 112 years. Soon it will be a housing estate. Nevertheless, the club endures, and at a new stadium perhaps our dreams will nearly reach the sky. We might have said goodbye to Boleyn, but we won't forget.

PETE MAY
London, September 2016

1

MY WEST HAM FAMILY

THIS SEASON MY FAMILY WILL BE LOSING AN OLD FRIEND: West Ham's Boleyn Ground, commonly known as Upton Park. The club is moving to the Olympic Stadium at Stratford. At the end of the 2015/16 season, the old ground will be turned into flats and part of my family history will be erased. Once, families had village churches to bind them together, now they have football stadiums. Three generations of my family have been Irons supporters, mainly through my – possibly misguided – influence.

When I started going to matches at the age of eleven in 1970, my dad Dennis (who had previously shown no interest in the game) and I stood on the cavernous terrace of the North Bank. Before kick-off, we bought paper bags of Percy

Dalton's roasted peanuts, still in their shells, from a man wearing a white coat. Our position was just behind the right goalpost, from where you could see the sweat on Bobby Moore's forehead and smell the Ralgex on the players' legs. For a suburban Essex boy, it was astonishing to watch the police chucking out swearing skinheads in high-leg DMs. Even the adults were calling Leicester's Frank Worthington a wanker. It was dangerous urban territory.

My dad became a convert and attended matches on his own after I started to go to games with my teenaged friends. But we'd often meet on the District Line home and after evening games share a pint in Upminster. You could sometimes see my dad's white summer jacket behind the goalpost on *The Big Match* after Sunday lunch. We both saw West Ham win the FA Cup at Wembley in 1975 and 1980. As my dad got older, he moved to a seat in the East Stand. Football became welcome neutral territory during my teenage years as we clashed over politics and his desire for me to go into farming. If nothing else, we could always discuss the length of Bobby Ferguson's goal kicks.

My mum Sheila only ever went to one game with us and was appalled by the swearing, but dutifully took an interest in the results. In 1986, when my parents moved to Norfolk, I took over my dad's season ticket in the East Stand and it felt like an initiation into adulthood.

When I became a parent myself, it was time to introduce my children into the Upton Park cult. The key, I thought, was not to force them to support West Ham, but to take them to easier, kids-for-a-quid home matches and hope they became fans by osmosis. I convinced my wife Nicola – who strangely prefers watching dressage to football – that it was a form of childcare.

My elder daughter Lola went to her first game when she was nearly five. She was entertained with 'sloppy egg, chips and beans' in Ken's Café on Green Street and then wine gums during the match. Using all my parental discretion, I explained that the chant the fans were singing was actually, 'You dirty northern custards!' She asked a lot of intelligent questions, such as, 'Daddy, why is he saying West Ham are useless?' and whether, if a defender took out a ladder and put the ball on the roof, it would be a yellow card.

I remember taking my younger daughter Nell to a game on her sixth birthday and her tears when West Ham lost at home to Watford, only to be pacified by a new Hammers hoodie from a stall in Green Street. She asked why they were calling Marlon Harewood 'an anchor' when he missed a penalty. We played like anchors quite often that season, though when I confessed that we were definitely going down, Nell insisted we'd survive and we did indeed pull off an incredible escape. At other games, fired up by primary-school mathematics classes, she'd speculate that West Ham would win 'infinity-nil'. It would certainly boost our goal difference, I suggested.

When they were younger, the girls sent me touching cards commiserating relegations and congratulating West Ham on play-off wins. Young Lola asked if I'd be sold too after one painful relegation, while Nell cried when Alan Pardew was sacked, believing that he had literally been placed in a sack. Best not give the chairman ideas, I thought. When she was ten, Nell sent her favourite player, Robert Green, an eloquent letter asking him not to leave. He ignored it and was subsequently relegated with Queen's Park Rangers.

At Ken's Café, Carol behind the counter always had a word for my daughters as they took their numbered tickets. Our trips were combined with a visit to the Newham Bookshop, where we bought *Horrid Henry* and *Diary of a Wimpy Kid* books, and to the Who Shop in Barking Road, which sold *Doctor Who* Lego figures and had a museum of props and costumes, entered through the door of the TARDIS. When we stayed late, we'd occasionally see star players driving off in Chelsea tractors with dark-tinted windows.

As well as these fond memories, the Boleyn Ground is mingled with memories of my parents' deaths too. While my mum was in hospital in King's Lynn, a UEFA Cup tie against Palermo at Upton Park provided welcome normality after a week of hospital visits. She had just been moved from intensive care, but, two days later, had died suddenly. On Boxing Day 2006, I took my dad, now eighty, to his final home defeat against Portsmouth. When I was at his bedside after a sudden stroke the following year, I was at least able to tell my dying father that West Ham had won a League Cup tie against Bristol Rovers, though typically our latest signing, Kieron Dyer, had been crocked. Talking about West Ham and Bobby Moore felt more comfortable than any deathbed confessions.

Despite the fact they've never seen West Ham win a major trophy, my teenaged daughters have continued to attend games at Upton Park, singing 'I'm Forever Blowing Bubbles' at kick-off and enjoying the fine cuisine of Ken's Café. 'Dad, have West Ham been replaced by aliens?' asked sixth-former Lola, not unreasonably, when we raced into a two-goal lead against Liverpool last season. Fourteen-year-old Nell was impressed to meet Trevor Brooking, a star from 'the olden days' before mobile phones, in the Newham Bookshop. After matches, she wonders why the carpets in the Boleyn pub are always sticky with beer.

Ironically, my daughters were more opposed to the stadium move than I was, and for all my arguments about improved transport links in Stratford they can perhaps sense their childhood – and the forbidden food of Ken's Café – fragmenting on the altar of increased match-day revenue figures.

Will it be the same in Stratford, even if we are playing next to the Westfield shopping centre, which my younger daughter loves? Lola will be on her gap year, but I've managed to get Nell a bargain £99 under-sixteen season ticket. Even so, long after Upton Park has become a housing complex, there will be part of London E13 that remains for ever West Ham in my family. The memories of skinheads on the North Bank, peanut sellers, dodgy chants, fry-ups, the odd glorious victory, home defeats and missed penalties will take a lifetime to fade and die.

And now the 2015/16 season is kicking off. West Ham are leaving the old, cramped, working-class streets of Upton Park for something grander, but perhaps less enticing and more corporate. We have a new manager and almost a new team.

As the writer David Goldblatt says, the stories that have been passed down about past teams and players are all part of football's shared cultural capital. I'm part of a wider family – one that embraces the strange sense of kinship that unites the followers of a perennially underachieving team playing at the Boleyn Ground. So let's give the old place a decent farewell.

2

IS THAT ALL WE BRING AT HOME?

WE ARE WEST HAM'S CLARET-AND-BLUE ARMY. SUMMER division. There can't be many other clubs that would get a crowd of 33,048 for a game against European minnows on 16 July. It's astonishing to see Green Street, E13, packed with so many fans. We're here for a Europa League Second Qualifying Round game. West Ham United against a side of Maltesers. Always thought the close season was overrated.

The club's website already has a 'countdown to history' widget, counting down the days until the move to the Olympic Stadium. This is how West Ham's final season at the Boleyn Ground begins – not with a bang, but Birkirkara FC.

It's not even West Ham's first game of the season. That was

a 3-0 win against Andorran minnows FC Lusitans on 2 July, which attracted a capacity crowd of 34,966. I'd missed that one due to family commitments; my elder sister Pam was over from Australia and had unaccountably booked her ten days in England, including a family stay in Norfolk, without considering the chances of West Ham qualifying for the UEFA Europa League Qualifying Rounds via the Fair Play league.

Admittedly, the tickets tonight are only a tenner for adults and a fiver for kids. But it's basically West Ham's reserves, kids and players returning from injury against a team no one's heard of in a glorified pre-season friendly. We're not Man United, Manchester City or Chelsea, and we haven't won a major trophy since 1980. But still they come...

One of the papers has pointed out that it was 30 July when West Ham won the World Cup in 1966 – that's two weeks after today's date. Domestic football shouldn't be played this early, but the astonishing loyalty of the West Ham fans proves the immense potential of this club. We need another 20,000 members of the claret-and-blue army for the move to the Olympic Stadium next summer, but judging by these summer gates it's going to be easy.

It's been a summer of change at West Ham. Sam Allardyce has not had his contract renewed after four relatively successful years, during which the club won the Play-Off Final and finished tenth, thirteenth and twelfth in the Premier League.

Yet, a large section of West Ham fans was never prepared to tolerate Big Sam's gruff demeanour, lack of PR skills or what they perceived to be his basic football style. Allardyce was a kind of footballing Thomas Gradgrind, always quoting results, results, results. Last season saw a great start, with the club fourth at Christmas. But the poor post-Christmas results that saw the Irons slump to twelfth place have given co-chairmen David Sullivan and David Gold the opportunity to act and appoint Croatian Slaven Bilić, a popular former player, as the new gaffer.

Bilić immediately showed himself to be a better PR man than Allardyce when he said: 'I remember West Ham as a special club … this is a cult club.' Another shrewd move was appointing his old teammate and club legend Julian Dicks, currently managing West Ham Ladies, to his coaching staff.

With a degree in law and the ability to speak four languages, Bilić is an academic at the Academy. In other ways, though, it's also a risky appointment, having let go of a manager who would have surely kept us up before the big move.

Bilić starts knowing that he wasn't the board's first choice. Rafa Benítez was said to be hours away from taking the job before Real Madrid intervened and took him to the Bernabéu. It's likely that Bilić also ranked behind some of the board's other rumoured targets: David Moyes, Carlo Ancelotti, Jürgen Klopp and Unai 'Dick' Emery.

Slaven undoubtedly has a fine record in his seven years' managing Croatia, although that, of course, did not involve buying and selling players. His club record is more worrying. His year at Lokomotiv Moscow saw him sacked after the side's worst finish (ninth) since the break-up of the Soviet Union in 1991, and he followed that by two seasons of finishing third at Beşiktaş in Turkey.

On a more positive note, he's played for West Ham under Harry Redknapp and was a great defender, though he did leave for the chance of more trophies at Everton. Nearly all the fans will be behind him, at least initially. We won't have a club at war with itself any longer or endless rancour between the pro- and anti-Sam brigades on social media.

Another plus is that Bilić has played guitar in his own rock band, which makes him a little cooler than Big Sam. He once said he wanted Beşiktaş to be 'as exciting as Iron Maiden'. When playing for West Ham, rather than visit Romford dog track, he preferred to fly to America to see Guns N' Roses. Slaven might also be able to provide some new heavy metal CDs for the match-day announcer to play at half-time instead of 'If the Kids Are United' and 'Twist and Shout'.

In Turkey, he liked to hang out with the Beşiktaş Ultras and was carried shoulder-high to the airport by them when he left. My fellow season-ticket holder Fraser did offer to carry Big Sam to Heathrow, though possibly not for the same reasons. Bilić clearly knows how to keep his fan base happy and is unlikely to cup his ear to the crowd, as Big Sam infamously did against Hull City.

Beşiktaş finished third in both his two seasons, though they looked like winning the league for a long period before fading, possibly through fatigue. Bilić also made a point of promoting young Turkish players at Beşiktaş; a similar policy with young English players would go down well at Upton Park.

Clearly Bilić has great charisma and beats Big Sam on connecting with the fans. Emotionally, too, he seems a good fit. At forty-six, Slaven should be coming into his peak years as a manager and you can't discount his fine record as Croatia coach. He's a good man-manager and will not be under huge pressure at West Ham. The board have set him the task of a top-ten finish, which is hopefully achievable. Nevertheless, it could be an interesting ride.

The appointment of Bilić marks the start of significant transfer activity. Midfielder Pedro Obiang arrives from Sampdoria, having been targeted by the board before the arrival of Bilić. Next to arrive is Marseille midfielder Dimitri Payet, who has fifteen caps for France and had twenty-one assists in the French league last season. Payet is twenty-eight, which means his resale value will be limited, but he sounds like a proper West Ham player.

The next big-money signing is the £10 million Juventus centre-back Angelo Ogbonna. Ogbonna is an exciting signing as he has ten caps for Italy and was an unused substitute in the Champions League Final against Real Madrid, though where he would fit in alongside Tomkins, Reid and Collins is unclear. Another crucial move is getting Arsenal's Carl Jenkinson on a second year's loan at right-back. Birmingham's goalkeeper Darren Randolph arrives as cover for Adrián, while another signing is promising Argentine playmaker Manuel Lanzini, loaned from UAE side Al Jazira.

So here we are in Ken's Café, awaiting my first game of the season. Fans queue at Carol's counter to make their orders and in turn receive the golden tickets of E13 that signal a passport to sausage, egg, chips and beans in twenty minutes' time. On the walls are fading pictures of old West Ham teams, price lists and a set of replica pistols.

Here is my team that meets in caffs. My fellow season-ticket holders include Matt, a vicar's son who has a most ungodly attitude to referees. He takes his partner Lisa on mini-breaks to places like Wigan and Bolton, where West Ham happen to be playing. Matt loves football stats, obscure football facts and visiting grounds like the Dripping Pan at Lewes.

We're joined by Nigel, who has been to all ninety-two Premier League and Football League grounds, completing the set with a trip to Fleetwood. Nigel is one of the Kew Gardens

Irons (possibly the only one) and an unlikely heavy-metal fan who's been obsessed with West Ham ever since his days at Brentwood School. He rivals Matt on the football trivia and Fantasy League front and hails from my home town of Brentwood.

Fraser has been going to games since before the Big Bang and once provoked a chant of 'There's only one Adam Faith!' from the West Ham fans during an away Intertoto Cup game. He has an enviable ability to keep calm during matches and likes to look at the big picture (which he often framed without Sam Allardyce). After epic victories, he likes to smoke a cigar for each goal.

Michael the Whovian is not just a *Doctor Who* aficionado, as he often points out, but more of a renaissance fan – though he did spend a lot of time drinking with the Brigadier from *Doctor Who*, aka Nicholas Courtney. Michael is also a playwright, politico and theatre-lover, as well as a man who remained permanently frustrated by Ricardo Vaz Tê. He's very proud of having Jonathan Spector's autograph. Michael buys everything on special offer in the Hammers store, including one memorable purchase of a West Ham dog bowl, even though he doesn't own a dog.

Sitting at a Formica-topped table covered in sauce bottles, Matt is causing a Twitter storm by revealing that I'm wearing my nineteen-year-old Dagenham Motors West Ham shirt as a tribute to Slaven Bilić. It also has the advantage of being relatively cool on a sweltering summer night. Matt claims it's the newest item in the May wardrobe. This is coming from a man in a 'lucky' Dukla Prague away shirt (he's a fan of Half Man Half Biscuit) that has so far seen us relegated at Wigan and a 0-9 aggregate defeat at Man City in the League Cup. And it's the same yellow and red as the kit Birkirkara are wearing.

We wonder if Carol behind the counter has the iced lattes ready and the air conditioning on. 'That would be Billy (Carol's grandson) waving a rolled-up copy of the *Standard*,' suggests Matt. Carol, with her blue apron and forceful personality, is something of a legend.

She's been on the counter forever, dispensing numbered tickets, admonishing those who don't hear the cries of 'Sixty-eight! I'm not telling you again! Sixty-eiiiight!', instructing her army of children and grandchildren to collect the empty cups, telling us it will be twenty minutes' wait for hot food and generally running the front of house better than any maître d' in the West End.

In an attempt to prove the pun is mightier than the sword, Michael the Whovian suggests that young full-back Lewis Page, who played against Lusitans, is always getting turned. I suggest he should be booked. We're joined by a full house of Lisa and Nigel's friend Gavin, also known as The Gav, plus tardy political correspondent Nigel, who has just raced here from the taxi in which the Lib Dems held their leadership contest.

As Michael consumes his first big breakfast of the season (with specially sautéed mushrooms from Carol) and Matt and Lisa (fresh from the Helsinki derby on their European mini-break) opt for cheesy chips, I'm not sure what the summer games will do for our health.

The West Ham team comes through on our mobiles. At least we've got our pre-season striker crisis in early. Sakho is suspended, Carroll is injured and Valencia has only just returned from the Copa América. So we're down to Modibo Maïga (remember him?), who was on loan to Metz all last season.

We hastily eat our chips and make our way to the Boleyn Ground. It's an expectant crowd. West Ham fans like European football. It's invariably something fleeting in E13, a moment that has to be cherished, even if this time it's against a bunch of Maltesers. Perhaps it all goes back to a magical night at Wembley in 1965, when West Ham actually won a European trophy, the Cup Winners' Cup, beating 1860 Munich with a classic display of passing and inventive football from a team of home-grown local stars.

Tonight's programme cover is a facsimile of the 1975/76 season, when West Ham reached the Cup Winners' Cup Final, only to lose 4-2 to Anderlecht. European nights at Upton Park were marked with special claret-and-white programme covers. These tended to get quite dirty in your pocket and the reproduction cover has some pleasingly authentic computer-generated black stains on it.

The Irons produced some memorable nights that season, such as the semi-final win against Eintracht Frankfurt, played before 39,000 fans crammed into the Boleyn Ground. Trevor Brooking scored the first with an unlikely header, Keith Robson appeared to have turned away from goal but then delivered a sumptuous thirty-yarder for the second. The classiest goal was Trevor Brooking's third, with Trev spinning to send a defender halfway towards Frankfurt and then calmly slotting the ball home at the South Bank end, before running to the West Side fans with his arm in the air looking like a man waving goodbye to a maiden aunt at Shenfield station. Though it has to be pointed out that WHU were disgracefully bad in the league that season; distracted by Europe, they didn't win any of their final sixteen games. With West Ham, there's always a caveat.

In 1981, Dinamo Tbilisi appeared to be a team of Supermen, firing home unstoppable goals and outplaying the Hammers in a 4-1 win at Upton Park. What was most memorable, though, was the way the home crowd applauded the Soviet side from the pitch. This was at the height of the Cold War and English football hooliganism. The Irons were greeted with a 'Welcome to West Ham: sportsmen of England' banner when they played the second leg in Tbilisi.

In more recent Premier League decades, there have been fewer European nights; but I recall Paolo Di Canio doing everything but score in a goalless draw against Dinamo Bucureşti in the UEFA Cup during the Harry Redknapp years.

In 2006, after a week of visiting my mum in hospital in King's Lynn, I travelled down to London for a UEFA Cup tie against Palermo. My mum had just been moved from intensive care, but died two days later. My mind wasn't on the game, but despite playing in pink, Palermo beat us 1-0 and won the return leg 3-0. And that was West Ham's last venture into continental football.

Now we're back in Europe through the back door of the Fair Play league and it's six games just to qualify for the tournament proper.

We take our seats in the East Stand. The game is predictably one-way in the first half. Maïga, Cresswell and Nolan go close. Maïga, who looks a bit stronger these days, is proving a nuisance, and near the break hits the post with a fine effort from the edge of the box.

We lose momentum in the second half. Zárate looks busy and wants the ball, but when he over-elaborates and is tackled, the Maltesers break and Liliu fires just wide.

Kevin Nolan, seen as Big Sam's talisman, goes off and the first – rather unfair – boos of the season can be heard around Upton Park. 'Is it too early to shout "Bilić out"?' I joke to Fraser.

Young Norwegian Martin Samuelson, signed from Man City's youth team, comes on for Amalfitano and plays it simple on the left. He doesn't look like he wants to take on his man, but displays a good touch on his competitive debut. Bilić makes a Big Sam-style substitution, taking off Maïga and replacing him with the diminutive Elliot Lee when surely we need two strikers on against a team that has parked the bus. Plut comes on for the Birks, providing some mild amusement in the week that Pluto was photographed (will they find some of Gary Strodder's clearances on the surface?). Ten minutes before the end, a row of eight fans in front of us all leave. Clearly they don't know West Ham.

After ninety minutes, it looks like we're going to face a Cup Final in Malta. Thankfully, Mystic Matt moves into action as Samuelson wins a corner. 'Our corners have been terrible all night and look at that, that's another poor one...' – only the keeper lets the ball sail over his head and Tomkins chests home. Never in doubt.

A poor game against limited opposition, but in what still feels like a pre-season friendly we've got a win and there's the likes of Kouyaté, Payet, Ogbonna, Obiang, Valencia,

Jenkinson, Sakho and Carroll to return. Though Nigel thinks I'm being Panglossian, whoever he played for.

We head off to the Central in Barking Road where, in what is normally a craft beer desert, they have finally stocked up on bottles of Old Speckled Hen. Nigel brings in a life-threatening chicken and chips takeaway, Matt asks questions about a Herzog film (strangely the woman walking through the pub selling dodgy DVDs doesn't have it) and, buoyed by a spirit of summer lightness, we drink three rounds. As we leave, the staff at the Central are setting up the breakfast tables for the hostellers staying above the pub – who says West Ham won't be putting up the Birkirkara players in style? Seems like our lucky vintage West Ham and Dukla Prague away shirts have finally worked their magic. Just.

A week later, West Ham manage to lose 1-0 in Malta and only get through to the next round after a penalty shoot-out, with young Diego Poyet scoring the decisive penalty. So we're back at Upton Park on Thursday 30 July for the third qualifying round against FC Astra of Romania. New signing Dimitri Payet is making his West Ham debut and slowly we're getting towards seeing a full-strength team.

The Ashes are still on, but football's coming home to E13…

It's another packed summer house as we anticipate the game in Ken's Café. The unusual name of FC Astra Giurgiu has special meaning for Whovians such as myself and Michael. Michael impersonates Tom Baker, once married to Lalla Ward, who played Princess Astra in *Doctor Who*. Meanwhile, Matt employs complex negotiating skills with Carol to pre-order a 7.45 p.m. takeaway portion of chips for the late-arriving Lisa. Nigel's absent as his mum is visiting and for some reason she doesn't want to see the best the Europa League has to offer.

We enter the East Stand, where we're joined by Fraser. It's West Ham pressure throughout the first half and we're starting to get a glimpse of what a Bilić team will look like. The wingers have gone and it's left to the full backs and Zárate and Payet to drift wide. Everything revolves around Dimitri Payet and he looks a real West Ham-type player, a scurrying presence with great skill and crossing ability who dominates the game going forwards. We also get to see young Reece Oxford playing as a holding midfielder. He plays it simple and looks remarkably composed for a sixteen-year-old. Unlike Big Sam, Bilić is clearly willing to play the kids.

West Ham take the lead after twenty-three minutes. A corner is half cleared, Payet jinks inside and outside his man on the left and delivers a perfect cross for Enner Valencia to rise well and score. That should be good for Enner's confidence, as he just didn't score enough last season.

The only Astra threat is when Joey O'Brien is pickpocketed by Budescu, who creates a chance. Yet our injury crisis has already begun to worsen. O'Brien has to go off with hamstring trouble after thirty-six minutes and is replaced by Reece Burke. A minute later Valencia goes down heavily and is stretchered off. On comes Modibo Maïga. It looks bad and there seems to an unwritten rule that all West Ham's three strikers have to be either injured or suspended. West Ham, though, still continue to attack and go close when Zárate, marginalised by Sam Allardyce and then injured while on loan at QPR last season, has a fine effort tipped away from the top corner.

The second half starts off well, and West Ham double their lead on fifty-one minutes. Zárate receives the ball halfway inside the Astra half and runs at three defenders. It looks like he will maybe pass to Maïga, but instead he bamboozles three defenders in a mazy dribble and prods the ball into the net. He's starting to look a player. Best goal of the season so far. 'SUPER SUPER SLAV … SUPER SLAVEN BILIĆ!' salutes the Bobby Moore Stand, having failed to sing Sam Allardyce's name for four years.

Still, at least we haven't quite forgotten how to mess up a two-goal lead. James Collins is booked for a body check and a few minutes later makes a silly challenge outside the area and receives a second yellow. That's the same Collins who in that day's *Evening Standard* warned about the dangers of WHU getting players sent off.

So it's down to Reece Burke at right-back and sixteen-year-old Reece Oxford at centre-back for the last thirty minutes. Oxford makes a couple of great interceptions and Ogbonna performs a saving tackle, but Astra pull one back with a thunderous first-time strike from the edge of the box from Boldrin.

Everyone starts to get nervous and we worry about Bilić's tactical acumen as he brings on Matt Jarvis for Zárate, rather than solidifying the midfield with Poyet or Nolan. The inevitable happens on eighty-two minutes. Ogbonna lunges at a pass into the box and manages to loop the ball up over Adrián into the top corner. Not quite as good as James Collins's effort at Man City, but as own goals go a bit of a classic.

To round the evening off, Maïga gets booked for diving and the ref ostentatiously delivers a red card to Bilić for something he said from the bench. Apparently it's quite common for Slaven to get sent off. 'You've got problems when Julian Dicks is on the bench telling you to calm down,' suggests Matt.

At least we don't actually lose. Matt texts Nigel to say that all he's missed is a two-goal lead overturned, Payet's debut, two red cards and an own goal. We retreat to the Central for a bottle of cold Old Speckled Hen. Matt suggests that our squad is starting to look a bit like Zola's: lots of good footballers but too many number tens in Payet, Zárate and Lanzini.

'It's July and we're already depressed,' I venture. We agree on the need for a striker like Charlie Austin, though for some reason the Vicar's Son ridicules my suggestion that Rickie Lambert might be a cheap fix for one season. There's some mirth at the *Daily Mail*'s report that the departed cult hero Carlton Cole is facing a driving ban for failing to identify who was driving his car when it was clocked speeding in London. Michael suggests that there are 30,000 character witnesses at Upton Park who will vouch that he's never been spotted going too fast in E13.

The Central then delivers a masterclass in how to empty a pub. We've waited ages to be served and then at 10.30 p.m. they play horribly loud music with vertebrae-shattering bass notes to drive us out. We leave via the gents' loos, which have flooded and look like something Bear Grylls would wade through.

Still, it's been an entertaining game, I reflect on the walk to Upton Park Tube through the darkened streets. We played well for sixty minutes and Sakho will be back for the second leg. But you sense this might be the end of our European tour.

'We'll concentrate on the League Cup,' suggests Fraser. 'That's the really big one.'

Before the return leg, my posse of fans become 'founders' of the new Olympic Stadium. We have an appointment at the Reservation Centre at Stratford's Westfield and as lead booker I feel a bit like Labour's Jeremy Corbyn, thrust into a leadership election by the paucity of credible candidates elsewhere. It's a heavy responsibility. There's been a late bid from my pal DC, once part of our East Stand enclave, to lure our group into the category A seats. After much consultation on what our core values are, this is turned down on a majority vote.

Matt, Nigel, Fraser and myself go along to the reservation centre at 7 p.m. for our Category B appointment. First we look at a computer-generated map of the stadium, and then view a video with a Ray Winstone uber-geezer voiceover. It feels a bit like we're buying a timeshare. Clearly you have to have a very deep voice to get a seat at the OS. Our adviser, Josh, a bearded WHU hipster, then shows us various options and views on the computer.

It all looks great. 'Just one thing,' asks Fraser. 'Do we have to watch West Ham? Might Barcelona be available?'

The options of stands and prices are confusing, but we end up going for seats at the front of the upper tier of the East Stand. They're roughly level with the edge of the penalty area and look as if they are close to the action, but also offer an aerial view of the overall play. We also buy for my daughter Nell (a bargain £99), Michael the Whovian, my old

Essex school friends Alison and Steve (who is coming up from Cornwall for games) and Alison's son Scott.

The Olympic Stadium will certainly be different to any other stadium. Because it's shaped like a bowl, the seats towards the corners are actually a bit closer to the pitch than the halfway-line seats.

So it's finally happening. After the reservation session we take on the really important business of assessing Stratford's boozers. First we try the Tap East in Westfield, which serves a nice pint of Red Atom real ale and a bottle of Belgian Duval for Nigel. It does food too, but is very small and doesn't look like it will cope with 54,000 lairy Irons fans singing 'Big Fat Frankie Lampard!' and spraying beer over River Island shoppers.

We move on to the Builders Arms, which is a bit run down but spacious, and has bottles of Doom Bar, but no real ale on draught. Our next stop is the Princess of Wales in West Ham Lane. There's only one old bloke having a half and the barmaid looks very surprised to see three customers enter. But it has Doom Bar on draught and the wooden interior isn't bad, with lots of space for football fans. Several other pubs are in the vicinity, which we will need to research before the big kick-off.

The following Thursday, Slaven Bilić names a team of kids for the return leg at FC Astra. Young Argentine playmaker Manuel Lanzini scores three minutes into his debut, but we lose 2-1 and stumble out of Europe. So no more worries about Thursday night fixtures and long trips affecting our league form. Bilić has made a clear statement that he's prioritising the first game of the season away to Arsenal at the Emirates. But we never get anything there, do we?

We're on holiday in the Lake District for the Sunday match at Arsenal as the Premier League season opens on 9 August. Luckily it's raining and I persuade my wife Nicola that I should watch the game at the Churchill Inn in Ambleside with our dog Vulcan, while she goes to Wordsworth's Dove Cottage with my daughter Nell and her friend Fernanda. However, it takes a lot of persuasion to get the bar staff to put the game on a token screen as the other northern punters prefer the Middlesbrough game, complete with Stewart Downing in a red shirt.

Arsenal exert a lot of early pressure and hit the bar, and it looks like it'll be the usual away defeat. But the defence is resilient and young Reece Oxford is very composed in front of the back four. Payet whips in a fine cross that Sakho just fails to connect with. When Payet takes a free kick late in the half, Kouyaté beats a hesitant Cech to head home from the edge of the box. Blimey. It gets even better after the break. Zárate turns onto a half-clearance and fires in a swift shot that Cech is very slow to go down for and the ball nestles in the corner. Yes! Zárate runs to the delirious away fans as, unbelievably, we're two goals up. Is Cech a double agent for José? The Arsenal fans bury their heads in their books.

After last season's late mishaps, it's quite possible we'll blow it at the end, but even with Jarvis, Nolan and Maïga on we still play out time comfortably. The last match we won here was in the Great Escape season of 2006/07, when I gave keeper Robert Green ten out of ten in my fans' markings in *The Observer*.

It's been a fantastic performance from Reece Oxford on his Premier League debut. Payet has looked really classy in midfield and Ogbonna and Reid and latterly Tomkins have been immense at the back. Vulcan is now officially West Ham's lucky dog even if he has watched from under the table – which is sometimes the best place to watch WHU performances from, but not today.

I send a celebratory text to my oldest daughter Lola, who is on holiday with an Arsenal family in Cyprus and is being threatened with being thrown in the pool. Don't worry, Gunners fans – I'm sure you'll still stay up. Matt, Lisa, Fraser and Michael have watched at the Hole in the Wall at Waterloo and have kept in touch via disbelieving texts, while Nigel messages, 'We just need another 37 points now.'

I celebrate with a chocolate cigar from one of Ambleside's many confectionary shops and a circular walk to High Sweden Bridge with my family followed by a pint of Hartley's XB. Who needs the Europa League? What a start.

We arrive back in London from the Lakes the following Friday night and the next day I'm on the Metropolitan Line Tube from King's Cross to Upton Park.

As the Tube arrives at Upton Park there's sense of sadness at the thought that this is the last time we'll be starting a season at the Boleyn. And does the clock still stand at ten to three, Rupert Brooke style? No, the sexist 'Don't kill your wife, let us do it!' sign above the dry cleaners in Green Street has lost its clock face entirely, as if time has stopped altogether in E13, which is probably a matter for Michael the Whovian. It's been there since I saw my first match in 1970 as a politically incorrect fixed point to my footballing life.

Little has changed; the chip shop by the Tube; the Queens pub, where I foolishly tried to get to the bar in my early days as a young fan and which featured on national TV when Millwall fans rioted in 2009; the Upton Park hardware store; No. 442 Green Street, where chairman David Gold grew up; the *Clockwork Orange*-style brutalist concrete of Queen's market, which is now a great source of spices, fruits and the one-pound fish man; Percy Ingle's bakery; Ken's Café; and what *On A Mission* fanzine editor Shane Barber christened, 'the Beirut flats' behind the market, which seemed to be forever burnt out in the 1990s.

And the thought occurs: have I wasted my life? For forty-five seasons I've been coming to around twenty games a season at the Boleyn. Could I have written the great novel without the distraction of football? Might I have lived as an expatriate, been a war correspondent (Millwall was pretty close), drunk decent beer instead of ending up in the Central, basked under the midnight sun on the northern fringes of Norwegian fjords, seen attack ships on fire off the shoulder of Orion… Might I, like Ian Dury, have been the ticket man at Fulham Broadway station? What a waste…

But no, West Ham has given me something constant. A place to go when sacked, dumped and unemployed, a refuge from parental and personal mortality and an alternative to mindfulness in that I can clear my brain of all other thoughts for ninety minutes. I've never had any thoughts of suicide because there's always another game to look forward to (or dread). I've listened to 35,000 fans telling Chelsea to stick their blue flag up their arse, seen Di Canio's goal against Wimbledon and learned that after years of misery occasionally things go right and 'Bubbles' wafts around the famous old stadium and we reach a Cup Final, stop Man United winning the league or stay up on salvation Sunday.

At the station I stumble into my old schoolmate Steve, who we've just signed up to sit with us at the Olympic Stadium. He still travels up from Cornwall for home games, a sign of the strange devotion our not-often-successful team inspires.

Inside Ken's Café, Matt and Lisa are attending their second game of the day, having already seen the under-eighteens at Little Heath and been in close proximity to young Martin Samuelson. While Michael is looking forward to *Bakkhai* at the Almeida, which is presumably some play about a Greek flat-Bakkhai four.

For some reason the club has designated it 'claret and blue day'. As the teams come on, claret and purple streamers cascade from above the stands. Are they the remnants of an Ann Summers' gift-wrapping outlet? One gets caught in the roof of the East Stand and stays there throughout the game.

West Ham have a decent first twenty minutes as a free kick from Payet sees Morgan head against his own bar and Sakho volleys over after a Zárate shot is blocked. But slowly Leicester come into it. Jamie Vardy is causing Jenkinson problems. The speedy striker is booked for clattering into Adrián but remains an irritant all game. On the other flank, Mahrez skins Cresswell and forces a good save from Adrián. The Hammers' custodian then makes a decent save from

Huth, only for the ref to give a goal kick. Adrián makes a 'shush' gesture to the Bobby Moore Stand, putting his finger to his lips, which gets a big laugh.

It all goes wrong on twenty-seven minutes. Reid doesn't get close enough to Vardy, who gets in a cross. Young Oxford has lost Okazaki and the Japanese striker produces a brilliant back-heeled volley. Adrián saves but the new City striker reacts well to head the rebound home. Quite an ironic combination, considering Vardy's recent apology for 'a regrettable error of judgment' in referring to a customer as a 'Jap' after an argument at a casino.

Ten minutes later, West Ham are 2-0 down as Albrighton gets down the left and despite five defenders in the box Mahrez arrives to fire home. 'We're Leicester City, we're top of the league!' chant the away fans. That will never last.

West Ham rally a little before the break. Payet plays in Sakho, who lobs wide, but is also brought down by Schmeichel's outstretched arm. It could easily be a penalty but the ref waves play on.

Bilić takes Reece Oxford off at half-time and brings on Pedro Obiang. Oxford has done some good things, but at sixteen he's still learning. A 'Cologne Hammers' banner hangs from the Bobby Moore Stand and you wonder if they think it's worth the journey.

Obiang has a decent game and brings some good tackling

and pace to the holding role. The Irons look a different side with Zárate hugging the left touchline and Payet is much more influential. Zárate comes infield to find Noble, who crosses into the box. Payet's first shot is blocked, but Kouyaté plays the rebound into his path and the Frenchman side-steps a defender to curl in a classy goal. Suddenly the crowd are up again.

In a spell of sustained pressure, Zárate nearly scores the goal of the season after a mazy dribble, but takes on one man too many. Leicester still look dangerous on the break and Drinkwater should make it three when he fires over. Vicar's Son Matt has his first Premier League tirade of the season at the hapless Jenkinson: 'Don't foul him … He wants the free kick … F**king hell! How difficult is it for Jenkinson not to foul him?'

The dependable Huth – who looks horrible to play against but is always effective and was surely sold too soon by Stoke – clears everything at the back for City. West Ham's best chance comes when Payet's header finds Sakho and Schmeichel makes an instinctive save with his chest from Sakho's volley. There are only three minutes of added time, which is odd considering Leicester's time-wasting.

Adrián goes up for one final corner, leaving an empty goal, which seems an unnecessary risk. When the ball is cleared the Hammers' keeper lunges in foot up and boots Vardy in the chest. Adrián's eyes are on the ball, but it's a dangerous challenge by a player who's not used to being upfield and the ref has little choice but to send him off. So that's three games out through suspension. 'Let's hope Robert Green has his bags packed,' suggests Fraser, referring to a rumour that Greeny might be returning. Jenkinson has to go in goal for the last seconds, but doesn't have to make a save as the game ends in victory for the Foxes. Surely West Ham should be beating teams like Leicester, who were in the relegation zone for most of last season.

As I head towards East Ham Tube there's a familiar rumble of discontent that could have come after any home defeat of the last forty years. 'Typical West Ham … How can we beat Arsenal and lose to Leicester? … That was disgraceful … I bet Allardyce is sitting at home laughing…'

Defeats, they don't get any easier. I can still recall the fans trooping home like Vietnam War veterans after one home defeat to Middlesbrough in 1989, muttering: 'I didn't think they could shock me any more … It's worse when we play well … Classic West Ham…' Another memory is *Fortunes Always Hiding* fanzine editor Steve 'North Bank Norman' Rapport raging at the cosmos (and on-loan Ray Atteveld) like a latter-day Captain Ahab after a galling FA Cup defeat at home to Sunderland in 1992.

In truth, Leicester look a half-decent side, but West Ham

have struggled against the basic tactic of using Vardy's pace. The full-backs appeared poor defensively, although the second-half performances of Zárate, Obiang and Payet were encouraging. But Sakho was isolated up front and we still need reinforcements. Typically, we now have a self-inflicted goalkeeping wound. A definite reality check after the Arsenal win.

My family are off on our second holiday of the summer the following Tuesday as we take the Eurostar to Paris and then train it to Salzburg in Austria. We enjoy Fraulein Maria's *Sound of Music* bicycle tour of the city, looking at Captain von Trapp's house by the lake, Maria's nunnery, and much more. I'm looking forward to West Ham getting their first home win against newly promoted Bournemouth at Upton Park. Nigel is using my season ticket to take his wife CQ and has promised text updates to Austria.

On the morning of the match we take a spectacularly scary cable-car ride to the top of the Untersberg, an Alpine mountain that is just over 6,400 feet high. We have lovely soup with chives and cheese dumplings at the café up there and then walk to the summit for stupendous views of the Alps. The only problem is the news arriving from Blighty.

Like the Hammers, it seems I've peaked too soon, as we've been left with a first-half mountain to climb. 'West Ham 0 Cresswell 2' is Matt's verdict as our normally reliable left-back blunders for both Bournemouth's goals. 'West Ham is alive with the sound of mucus,' texts Nigel.

By the time we're back down from the Alps, West Ham have pulled back to 2-2 through an iffy Noble penalty and a Kouyaté goal. We'll surely go on to win it now. Then it's revealed that Jenkinson has been beaten far too easily as Pugh scores Bournemouth's third and the hapless Jenks is sent off for conceding a penalty. Callum Wilson makes it 4-2 from the spot and completes his hat-trick. Trust us to set up Bournemouth's season with their first-ever Premier League win.

'Both full backs have been abysmal,' is Matt's texted verdict. There's even more shocks when substitute Modibo Maïga scores his first goal in over a year for the Hammers to make it 3-4. 'That's how you get to be first on *Match of the Day*,' suggests Matt. 'If anyone tells you there were any positives for West Ham, take it with a pinch of Salzburg.' We have a corner cleared off the line but there's no late equaliser.

This is worrying. Bournemouth are a confident side and Wilson is a good striker; but after a great win at Arsenal we've lost two at home to lower-level teams. Bilić said he'd restore the West Ham way, but this is more reminiscent of the erratic form of Ron Greenwood's sides post-1966, winning friends and losing matches. The team will take time to gel, but even so, this result suggests a struggle.

It's hard to legislate for Cresswell and Jenkinson making such calamitous errors against Bournemouth. Both looked good players last season and will improve this time, but it's clear they need more support from midfield. Surely having seen what happened against Leicester, Bilić should have changed the narrow midfield diamond formation to something more like a conventional 4-4-2 or 4-5-1? Perhaps we're also missing Alex Song, who had such a fine first half of the season last time out, and Stewart Downing, now at Middlesbrough, who could stop out wide and play in the middle. The other worrying factor is that we have accrued endless silly red cards – so far Sakho, Tomkins, Collins, Adrián and Jenkinson have all been sent off, which shows a lack of discipline in the side.

Unlucky injuries, sendings off and home defeats is not a great recipe... The *Guardian* report of the Bournemouth match mentions the prospect of relegation, which is surely a bit premature, but the gamble of replacing Allardyce is looking a risk at the moment – Rafa Benítez was within three hours of taking the WHU job, claims the *Daily Mail*. Though we achieved a great win at Arsenal, Bilić and the team are still learning and should we get anything at Liverpool it will all look a lot better. Though not having won there since 1963, that's a big if…

We arrive back from our holidays to find that ageing skipper Kevin Nolan, the embodiment of the Allardyce years, has departed by mutual consent and Mauro Zárate has picked up an injury in training.

I listen to the match at Liverpool with a combination of BBC Sport updates and Radio London commentary. Liverpool have won their first three games. Incredibly, Cresswell crosses and Lanzini scores for West Ham after three minutes. Have we scored too early? This is surely where new signings Benteke, Firmino, Milner and Clyne will prove that Liverpool are a title-chasing force again. But no. On twenty-nine minutes, some poor play by Lovren lets in Lanzini, who dispossesses the defender and crosses from the by-line for Noble to stroke home. Two-nil to the Cockney Boys! It seems a 4-3-3 formation is working much better, with Lanzini and Payet supporting Sakho and Noble, Obiang and Kouyaté shielding the defence.

That two-nil half-time score has me thinking of the FA Cup Final, but this time we don't f**k it up. Liverpool's Coutinho is red-carded, but then it gets very worrying when Mark

Noble is also sent off, unjustly, with twelve minutes to go. I keep telling myself that even a point will be a good result as I sit powerlessly before the yellow logo of bbcsport.com. But Liverpool only have three real chances, with Firmino hitting the post, Milner blasting wide and Lovren hoofing over. In the second half, WHU keep going forward. Cresswell forces a save and Reid heads a good chance over.

Added time sees a flurry of West Ham corners. And then Kouyaté wins the ball for Sakho, who strokes the ball into the corner with a great finish. Yeeess!!!! My daughters wonder why I'm shouting in the office. 'We're winning 3-0 at Liverpool!' I declare, disbelievingly. You can hear some great chants of 'Diafra Sakho, he scores when he wants!' on the radio and then, 'We want four!' and 'Is there a fire drill?'

What a fantastic result when you consider West Ham were without Jenkinson, Adrián, Valencia, Zárate, Carroll, Collins and O'Brien and had Matt Jarvis babysitting a bunch of teenagers on the bench. The last time we won at Anfield was on 14 September 1963, when I was in very short trousers, *Doctor Who* was yet to be broadcast and the Beatles had just released their first LP. Time to 'Twist and Shout'!

Watching *Match of the Day* with a whisky, it's good to see Slaven Bilić mastering his English gaffer metaphors, saying, 'We parked the bus but we left the hand-brake off.' You wait fifty-two years for a win at Liverpool and then three goals and a bus with the handbrake off turn up. Leaving Liverpool looking like that bus at the end of *The Italian Job*.

MOTD singles out Lanzini for special praise and he did a great job harassing the Liverpool defence and tracking back on the right. Both red cards were harsh; Coutinho was flummoxed by a piece of Payet skill and Mark Noble was fouled and then played the ball – hopefully his sending off will be rescinded.

It's tough on my pal Big Joe, who texts to say that he's been going to Anfield for thirty years and never seen us win so much as a corner, but missed this one because his brother-in-law is on holiday.

Crisis, what crisis? Never in doubt we'd end our 52-year Anfield hoodoo by winning 3-0. What a bizarre season so far. Perhaps this is the West Ham way.

The occasion is so remarkable that Hammers fan Jon High becomes a social media star through tweeted pictures of the result tattooed on his leg.

August ends with transfer deadline day and West Ham make more progress. Nikica Jelavić, who played under Bilić with Croatia, is signed from Hull City to provide cover for the striking positions, while Alex Song, so influential last season, arrives for another season's loan from Barcelona. To solve the problem of a lack of width, in come Victor Moses (on loan from Chelsea) and the £7 million Michail Antonio, a powerful goal-scoring winger from Nottingham Forest, who is also, as far as can be ascertained, the first Shakespearian character from *Twelfth Night* ever to play for the Hammers.

It leaves most fans in danger of feeling optimistic. If nothing else, Sullivan and Gold's transfer spree should ensure we're still in the Premier League for the Olympic Stadium move and really it should guarantee a top-half finish. As September begins, we've only played four league games and six Europa League ties but it feels like we've been going for ever. West Ham have been knocked out of Europe, signed ten players, lost twice at home and won at Arsenal and Liverpool. What else might happen before we say goodbye to the Boleyn?

3

GOODBYE TO BOLEYN

FROM SEAT F212 IN BLOCK ES11 OF THE UPPER EAST Stand, I can gaze to my left at the nearby Bobby Moore Stand; the Betway Stand is across the pitch and at the far end of the stadium is the Sir Trevor Brooking Stand. After forty-six years of attending matches, every part of the stadium holds memories.

What is now the Sir Trevor Brooking Stand was once the North Bank. It was a cacophonous old barn really, just concrete steps with crush barriers, a rudimentary roof and broken peanut shells underfoot. To enter the North Bank, you'd go through the club's claret-painted iron gates in Green Street and turn left at the forecourt, often directed by a policeman on a horse. A long queue was always present at the 'BOYS/OAPs' half-price turnstile (girls didn't seem to exist in West Ham's nomenclature). Back in 1972, it was 15p for boys and 30p for adults to stand on the North Bank. That's when David Bowie or Rod Stewart albums cost £1.99, so it was pretty good value.

Once you had clicked your way through, with a small *Hammer* programme in your pocket, there would be a stall selling Bovril away to the right, and ahead a mass of standing humanity. There was a man in a brown coat who'd walk around intoning in a nasal voice, 'Peanuts, peanuts, roasted peanuts!' He sounded like the sort of character Peter Cook might play. You'd buy the nuts in white paper bags, crack open the shells and throw them on the terraces. This left a crunchy, post-match carpet of nutty detritus.

Outside the ground there were lads dressed in white lab coats with the players' names written on them in felt pen. Some fans had claret-and-blue scarves around their wrists. The police were busy prodding the toes of leather boots and confiscating high-leg, steel-toe-capped Doc Martens from skinheads.

On either side of the terrace, at right-angles to the pitch, were curious raised mini-terraces referred to as the shelf or 'cage'. You had a great view of the goal but very little chance of seeing down the other end as you were standing at a ninety-degree angle to the posts.

At the back of the mass were mysterious chants of 'We've got 'Arry 'Arry 'Arry Redknapp on the wing!' Leicester's flamboyant striker Frank Worthington was greeted with 'Oh wanky wanky wanky, wanky wanky wanky Worthington!' After every goal youths would be led away by policemen, who held them in painful-looking arm locks. The Old Bill took these miscreants around the pitch and down the players' tunnel before expelling them from the ground.

Initially I stood behind the goal with my dad, at the front just behind the right-hand post. You could see the sweat on Bobby Moore's brow at corners. My dad, not the most sociable of men, got to know an East End mother and daughter who stood in front of him by the perimeter hoardings eating sandwiches and drinking tea from a Thermos flask. Sometimes he even drove them to away games.

Certain goals stick in the mind, like a diving header by the previously barracked Bobby Gould from a Frank Lampard cross. He scored in a 6-2 win over Leicester in 1974 – the Hammers had been a goal down early on – and Bobby celebrated right in front of me.

Brian Clough's Derby County visited in 1972 and the result was a thrilling draw. On a muddy, sanded pitch, West Ham levelled it with a delightful Trevor Brooking goal. He jinked past a couple of Derby defenders and curled the ball into the corner of the North Bank net to make it 3-3. There was something effortlessly classy about that movement as he ran away to celebrate, complete with his *Onedin Line* sideburns.

The roof had only been placed on the North Bank in 1961. With increasing age my position gravitated further towards the back of the North Bank. In the silly days of the 1970s, my friends and I would watch in safety as windmill-punching hooligans steamed into Man United fans at the far South Bank. We'd mutter knowingly about the ICF and the Mile End Mob.

Sometimes I'd leg it to Upton Park having played for my school football team in the morning, legs still muddy from firm but fair performances as a rugged centre-back.

While attending Lancaster University, I returned for games in the vacations, such as a home win against Chelsea in 1978. One of my old Essex pals managed to start a – not exactly Wildean – chant among the hard-core lads at the back, suggesting that a Chelsea player show us a personal part of his anatomy.

For ninety minutes David 'Psycho' Cross metaphorically stalked the showering Chelsea defence with a kitchen knife. The North Bank boomed in one ominous voice, 'Psychooooo! Psychooooo!' as Brooking, Green and Holland scored in a 3-1 win. Cross got stuck in and that's all anyone ever wanted.

In the next home game, a 3-0 win against Derby, a young centre-half called Alvin Martin took the eye with his calm approach to defending. Returning to Essex after university, I watched Jimmy Neighbour score the winning goal as West Ham overturned a first-leg deficit to win a League Cup semi-final and return to Wembley in 1981.

The North Bank was knocked down in 1995 and rebuilt as the Centenary Stand. One corner of the Centenary Stand was devoted to away fans, with the home fans now preferring the Bobby Moore Stand. It was in the Centenary that Man United fans sang, 'Giggs will tear you apart again…' and 'Where's your famous Danny Dyer?' Stoke fans wanted to know 'Why, why, why, Delilah?' and Chelsea fans unveiled 'Benítez out!' banners at their own manager in 2014 – one of the few occasions at the Boleyn when both sets of fans have been singing 'You're getting sacked in the morning!' in unison.

I sat in the Centenary Stand when my daughter Nell received two free Youth Academy tickets for West Ham versus Birmingham in 2008. It was Nell's seventh birthday; she had her picture in the programme and we heard announcer Jeremy Nicholas mention her name on the PA. West Ham at least avoided defeat, drawing 1-1 thanks to a very rare Freddie Ljungberg goal.

For much of the 1980s, my choice was the more sophisticated world of hard-core banter in the Chicken Run, the lower section of the East Stand. You'd walk to the Chicken

Run down Tudor Road and then through the alleyway by the bus depot into Priory Road, where for years a piece of 'Lyall out!' graffiti was left undisturbed.

When my dad moved to King's Lynn in 1986, I took over his East Stand season ticket for half a season and watched the Irons nearly win the league from the Upper East Stand. The next season it was back to the Chicken Run as I purchased a standing season ticket. It was the wittiest section of Upton Park; a place where you'd hear cries of 'Come on, Hammers, really pep it up and make it mediocre!'

We'd stand close to 'Lino', a bloke in a respectable suit with a particular gift for obscenely hollering at linesmen. The crowd were just feet away from the players and the poor linesman was constantly regaled with coruscating cries of 'Oi, lino!!!! F**king lino!' Lino's other target was the hapless Kevin Keen. Lino would exclaim at mind-numbing volume: 'Oi, Keen!! Put 'im under! Put 'im f**kin' under!!! For f**k's sake, put 'im f**kin' under!!!' Poor Kevin probably still awakes in a clammy sweat fearing he's still being told by Lino to 'put 'im under'.

It was on the Chicken Run that I met Steve Rapport, a bloke in a black leather jacket who would scream, Adrian Edmondson-style: 'Remember goals, West Ham? They were big in the '70s!' Steve went on to become North Bank Norman and edit *Fortune's Always Hiding* fanzine, which we'd sell from our stall in a front garden next to Ken's Café. Poor Steve was one of life's perfectionists. He should have been born in Barcelona, where he could have supported a truly great side; instead, the gap between his dreams and West Ham's often horrible reality was so great that he eventually, perhaps fearing football-induced spontaneous combustion, emigrated to San Francisco and started watching baseball – though he was still able to return for Boxing Day home defeats and periodically become incensed by Big Fat Sam on Facebook.

During the Redknapp years, my pal DC got together a group of like-minded season-ticket holders and we took seats in the Upper East Stand, in the corner facing the Bobby Moore Stand. These included Dan, who would bet on just about any possible score and went missing in action after conceiving a child in the mistaken belief that Paolo Di Canio's goal against Chelsea would keep us up in 2003; Steve and Jenny, who would unfailingly park in Hubert Road and arrive in the stadium with welcome bags of chips from the Ercan chip shop; young Joe O'Brien, whose leg room was severely compromised by Shane Barber, the editor of *On A Mission* fanzine; Shane's mate John and Martin, a bloke from Scotland, who only ever turned up for one match. Eventually Matt, Nigel and Fraser joined us and we stuck together even when DC, tired of running for the Silverlink, opted for the more modern attractions and better transport links of the brand new Doctor Martens Stand (later the Alpari and then the Betway Stand).

Every spot in the stadium has its characters. Like the bloke who used to sit in front of us in the East Stand. He had blond spiky hair, wore a medallion and always referred to Paulo Wanchope as 'the Chop' (as in, 'Go on, the Chop!'). He called Frank Lampard 'the Pie'. One unfortunate blonde woman was christened 'Colin Hendry' by our party after her striking resemblance to the Blackburn defender, while a very young blond boy became 'Freddie Sears', as the real-life footballer always looked about thirteen.

There are so many memories of sitting in the East Stand, not least the madness of a 5-4 win over Bradford City when Paolo Di Canio proved himself a fully fledged nutter. At 4-2, Paolo tried to sub himself after having his third penalty appeal turned down. Harry Redknapp persuaded him to return, then he wrestled the ball from Frank Lampard to score a penalty and inspired an astonishing 5-4 win. We had a great view of Joe Cole's winner at the Bobby Moore end. It's not often you see a striker with voices in his head and a grand operatic vision of redemption.

For sheer atmosphere, the play-off second leg against Ipswich in 2004 was hard to beat, from the moment the man with a horn came on and played the 'Post-Horn Gallop'.

When Jermain Defoe netted a late winner against Blackburn for our first home win of the season – in January 2003 – the scenes in the East Stand resembled VE Day. Or there was the time that snow caked a freezing Upton Park and Jonathan Spector suddenly played like Lionel Messi with an orange ball, as we demolished Man United 4-0 in the League Cup.

Some of my Essex gang started to stand in the South Bank in the 1970s and 1980s. There was a frisson of danger at being so close to the away fans, often only held apart by a line of police. One memory is of a fan who spent the whole game calling Nottingham Forest's Jim Barron 'Shitbag!' Poor Stan Bowles received a lot of comments about his wife too.

One goal at that end that I'll never forget was a glancing header by Bryan Robson against the eventual champions, Don Revie's Leeds. We beat them 3-1, fancy sock tags and all. At the end of the 1977/78 season, a huge skinhead sat sobbing with his head in his hands as West Ham were relegated after a home defeat by Liverpool.

My pal Steve was arrested after a goal surge against Notts County in 1978. He was then charged with assaulting a police officer as he was dragged out. In the subsequent court case my turn came as a star witness. The prosecution's case, probably compiled by Gene Hunt, was based on the fact we must have all been hooligans if we were standing in the South Bank. It claimed that Steve had tried to knee the policeman in the groin. From the witness box I was able to point out to the magistrates that Notts County had a very low average gate and were not renowned as troublemakers. The case was duly not proven, not least because the copper was much bigger than Steve.

In the 1980s, there was the less pleasant feeling of a fan on the South Bank indulging in some open-air urination and spattering the back of my jeans. He was big and drunk so I didn't say anything. At times in the early 1980s, British National Party supporters in green bomber jackets would sell copies of the newspaper outside.

For one sold-out game against Ipswich I even bluffed my way into the away end to get into the game. By 1986, there were worrying gaps in the South Bank as crowds slumped to new lows and the future of football itself was in question, at least until McAvennie and Cottee restored optimism and end-of-season full houses.

The only time I sat in the Bobby Moore Stand was with Philosophy Football's Mark Perryman and musical legend Billy Bragg. We'd been distributing cards on seats to make a giant England flag as part of England Fans United's Raise the Flag initiative. Eng-er-land lost 3-1 to Australia, but we did see Francis Jeffers score his only England goal.

Former match-day announcer Jeremy Nicholas once gave me a tour of his commentary box in the corner of the Bobby

Moore Stand and I almost found myself saying, 'We go above Tottenham!' before announcing that Mr Moon had left the stadium.

Otherwise I'll simply remember the Bobby Moore Stand as the place where all the good songs emanate from, such as, 'You're shit and you slap your bird!' aimed at Aston Villa's Stan Collymore and classics such as 'From Stamford Bridge to Upton Park, stick your blue flag up your arse!' and 'Oh, Christian Dailly, you are the love of my life!'

My first-ever match was watched from a seat in the West Stand with my dad in 1970. West Ham were, as ever, struggling against relegation and won 2-1. John McDowell was making his debut. Back then we feared football hooligans, having seen some scary stuff on *Play for Today*, and it took a few more games before we embraced the forbidding North Bank.

In later years, my friends tried the lower West Side. If you stood too far back the ball disappeared every time it went up in the air, obscured by the line of the upper stand. We stood on the West Side when Ray Stewart's penalty sent West Ham into the FA Cup semi-final on 1980 and chanted at the forlorn Brummies in the South Bank. Another memory of the Brentwood Irons was of a West Side 'character' who spent the whole game shouting 'Oi Spotty!!!' at Alan Curbishley until eventually throwing up over a crush barrier.

My dad and I stood on the West Side among the hardy souls who braved a snowstorm to see West Ham beat Cambridge 3-1 in 1979. At half-time Club DJ Bill Remfry played Mike Oldfield's '*In Dulci Jubilo*'. It inspired an unlikely prog-rock knees-up among the fans, who stamped their feet and shuffled from foot to foot as by this time they were experiencing frozen tubular bells. Bill Remfry was the sort of DJ who used to put the word 'rock' in inverted commas. The club built him his own box on the front of the stand. 'He looks just like Davros!' muttered my old school friend Paul Garrett, as we gazed at Bill's upper body emerging from his box, which may or may not have been fronted with Dalek bumps.

A couple of times Paul and myself made it into the press box for Milk Cup ties when I was working for the sponsors of the tournament, the National Dairy Council. It was a wondrous place, full of cubicles with clunky old mainline phones for delivering copy, a portly retainer dispensing sausage rolls, and lots of hacks in raincoats who looked like characters from *The Sweeney*. We saw West Ham beat Bury 10-0 and had to remember not to cheer. Despite it being a record home win, West Ham boss John Lyall was so impressed with Bury's bemused centre-back Paul 'Diego' Hilton that he bought him.

In 2001, the grand old West Stand was demolished and replaced with the giant Doctor Martens Stand, complete with mock castles at the front (very Essex) and a hotel facility. Strangely, the hotel idea never took off, despite the chance for customers to buy West Ham's own-label chardonnay and have a room overlooking the pitch.

I took my daughter Nell to a couple of games in the Doctor Martens Stand. As I mentioned in the opening chapter, on her seventh birthday she asked why they were calling Marlon Harewood 'an anchor' as West Ham lost at home to Watford. She cried when we lost, but was cheered up by a new West Ham hoodie. A happier occasion was seeing Sunderland dispatched 2-0 with goals from Stanislas and Tomkins as the Bobby Moore Stand chanted 'Dirty northern custards' (at least that's what I told Nell) at the Mackems.

For me, the West Side of the Boleyn will always be Bill Remfry and Mike Oldfield. Even the pitch itself has a few tales. The fanzine I was writing for, *Fortunes Always Hiding*, helped organise the anti-Hammers Bond protests in 1989, when the club was asking £500 for the right to buy a season ticket. There was a mass pitch invasion after a game against Wimbledon and banners reading 'Lying Thieving Cheats' were unfurled. For a time, it felt like being Lenin at the start of the Russian revolution; I was a little worried the fans would storm the boardroom and install Julian Dicks as the People's Commissar. As it was, we just settled for the dismantling of the Bond scheme.

Having been a fairly peripatetic spectator over the years, every side of the ground is steeped in emotion. Memories of the fans as much as the players, of matches past, of smells, sensations, comments and the fabric of London's social history. There will be more memories from this season, and then the ground will be a housing estate. And we'll have to say goodbye to Boleyn.

4

WE'VE GOT PAYET!

SEPTEMBER BEGINS WITH ONE OF THOSE TWO-WEEK international breaks that seem to take longer than a Tolstoy novel, when all Premier League life stops and we try to get excited about England playing San Marino. Club fans need results and statistics to ingest – without them we might overload like some tape-spilling computer in 1970s *Doctor Who*. To make the West Ham-free break even longer, the game against Newcastle is being screened on Sky on a Monday night, which means it's been sixteen days since our epic win at Anfield.

It's a kids-for-a-quid game so I opt to take my younger daughter Nell. We have a convoluted journey to Upton Park. The Hammersmith and City Line to Barking suddenly becomes a Circle Line train at Liverpool Street following a 'passenger incident at Upton Park'. So it's on to the packed Central, Jubilee and District Lines as we fear missing the deadline for dinner at Ken's Café, which is normally the highlight of our dad/daughter bonding.

Eventually we arrive at Upton Park station and on the walk past the Green Street dry cleaners I notice that not only has the clock been smashed but now the 'Don't kill your wife, let us do it!' sign has gone too, leaving just an empty oblong void. It feels like part of my footballing life has gone with that sexist sign. It had survived Germaine Greer, Spice-mania and Naomi Klein but had finally succumbed to pre-Stratford hubris. Brian Williams, the author of *Nearly Reach the Sky*, has travelled to the match by car, but later Facebooks me to learn if the news is true. He is equally distraught: 'Call me an old sceptic, but I doubt the person who smashed the clock face was striking a blow for feminism. It's as if something irreplaceable has been taken from us...'

In Ken's Café we find Lisa, dutifully waiting with a ticket for the Gav. Michael the Whovian is absent, watching Benedict Cumberbatch in some play called *Hamlet*. Meanwhile, Carol does her usual efficient job, serving Nell fortifying sausage, egg, chips and beans before kick-off and remarking on how big she's become. A flustered Gavin arrives five minutes before kick-off after problems on the A13.

Later it emerges that the Newcastle players have had terrible trouble parking the bus. They've had to walk the last mile to the stadium, meaning they now know how we felt during the 2010/11 season, when Upton Park station seemed permanently closed due to planned engineering works and we all had to yomp in from Canning Town, West Ham and Stratford. Still, at least the Toon lads had time to get a programme and some last-minute burgers from Green Street. Though they're not as late as Nigel, who eventually arrives forty-three minutes into the game, having been detained at the office.

We meet Fraser in the East Stand. I place my daughter in my seat – instructing everyone not to swear in front of minors – and take Nell's kids-for-a-quid seat in Row R at the very back of the stand. Some of Bobby Zamora's shots are probably still lodged up here. I've never sat so far back before. I'm sitting next to a metal stanchion and here you can't see the digital scoreboard and clock because of the low roof. Intriguingly, the back of our stand is a thin sheet of corrugated iron (or maybe corrugated Irons?). With a hefty push I'd probably fall into Priory Road.

The Olympic Stadium will hopefully be made of sturdier stuff, but it's also nostalgic to think that people sat here watching Moore, Peters and Hurst when the East Stand was built in 1968. Before that it was the old wooden Chicken Run.

There's some wonderful old *Match of the Day* footage of the three World Cup winners running out onto the pitch before a guard of honour to take the acclaim of both sets of fans against before the 1966/67 season's opening match against Chelsea. Moore, Hurst and Peters jog past the brass band, run towards the South Bank and salute the old Chicken Run. Though, this being West Ham, the Irons went and lost 2-1 to ruin the trio's homecoming.

The East Stand is now the oldest part of the Boleyn Ground and the only section that has remained unaltered since my first match in 1970.

We always seem to play well under the lights. It's a tradition that goes back to games like the League Cup tie against the then mighty Liverpool in 1989, when Paul Ince scored twice and Tony Gale curled in a free kick and we hammered them 4-1. Indeed, I once saw the Boys of '86 beat tonight's opponents 8-1 in a midweek game, with Alvin Martin scoring a hat-trick against three different keepers. Back when we looked on course to win the league. Will West Ham ever be in such a position again?

The game kicks off at 8 p.m. In the press, much has been made of the fact that it's the first time Slaven Bilić and Steve McClaren have competed against each other since Bilić's Croatia beat McClaren's England at Wembley in 2007.

Victor Moses gets a debut in place of Obiang and looks

instantly dangerous wide on the left. West Ham take the lead on nine minutes with a great goal. Sakho finds Noble with a back-heel and the new skipper rolls the ball into the path of Dimitri Payet. The Reunion man side-foots a brilliant finish into the top corner. Great composure from Dimitri. 'How shit must you be, we're winning at home!' chants the Upton Park crowd.

We play very well in the first half. Payet brings gasps of admiration from the crowd for some audacious pieces of skill; Moses looks much better than the player I remember on loan at Liverpool and Stoke; and Kouyaté dominates the midfield. Newcastle have a good chance when Janmaat gets through, but Randolph makes a decent save with his legs.

James Tomkins has deservedly kept his place at right-back and at one point plays a great pass out to the wing for Victor Moses. Even the departure of the injured Ogbonna doesn't affect the Hammers too much, as Jenkinson comes on and Tomka reverts to centre-back. The appearance of Andy Carroll on the touchline prompts a rousing chorus of 'He left 'cos you're shit!' at the Newcastle fans.

I manage to find a spare seat next to Fraser for the second half. The game is effectively over when a Newcastle free kick breaks down and Moses shows great pace to run from his own half and part the black-and-white sea. He cuts inside a defender and fires against the bar, but Payet is on hand to volley home with a finish that is more difficult than he makes it look. He celebrates by sucking his thumb. 'We'll miss him when he's gone in January,' suggests the fan next to me, only half-joking.

Payet looks to be the complete player. He always has time and can use his body to deceive players in a manner reminiscent of Trevor Brooking (though admittedly Trev never sported a semi-Mohican). Dimitri can effortlessly dribble through defences, finishes calmly and takes brilliant free kicks and corners. He might not be great in the air or at tackling, but as an offensive midfielder he looks like a superb buy.

West Ham play with pace and verve for the rest of the half, with Sakho, Payet and Moses combining well and a number of crosses causing consternation in the box. 'We're West Ham United, we play on the floor!' chants a disbelieving Bobby Moore Stand in a jibe at a certain past manager. And then it's a mischievous 'Down with the Chelsea! You're going down with the Chelsea!' aimed at the Geordies.

Three substitutions spark a small Newcastle revival and Randolph saves low from Janmaat and makes another good tip-over from a deflected de Jong shot. It's been an extraordinary week; first Jeremy Corbyn gets elected Labour leader and then Andy Carroll is seen on a football pitch. With two minutes to go, Big Andy comes on. He manages to risk both injury and a booking with a charge into Krul but thankfully survives intact.

We've finally won at home and it's a promising performance. 'They've got a long journey home,' remarks someone as we walk by the Newcastle coaches. 'Why do they come so far to watch their team lose?' asks fourteen-year-old Nell. 'She hasn't been watching us long,' chuckles a fan next to me, remembering our previous home games. But for once we've won fairly comfortably at Upton Park. Slaven has beaten the Wally with the Brolly again, we're playing good football and we're up to fifth. Now we just have to win at Man City.

A few days later, quite a few papers pick up on David Sullivan's admission in the Newcastle programme that West Ham are set to make a loss of between £10 million and £17 million, depending on our league position, following the summer's transfer deals. Though hopefully that loss might be negated by winning the Premier League, the FA Cup and League Cup, which often seems very likely after several pints of Maldon Gold in the Black Lion. Sullivan also wrote that the total salaries were at the limit of the financial fair play rules and that if there is any activity in January, West Ham would have to sell before they buy. Though hopefully that shouldn't be too big a problem, as West Ham now have two players for every position and the squad is looking extremely strong, with several promising youngsters coming through. The luxury item in our purchasing was probably Angelo Ogbonna, purchased for £8.5 million when the club already had Tomkins, Reid and Collins, though he's certainly added strength to the back line.

While West Ham play at Man City, we're on a Sunday afternoon family trip to Rainham Marshes. It's a saturated, boggy wasteland full of biodiversity, so not too different to the loos of certain pubs in E13... But after admiring the marsh frogs and egrets and then catching the Overground from Purfleet to Crouch Hill, I watch the first half from the Stapleton Tavern, which serves a very nice pint of Black IPA.

Astonishingly, West Ham go ahead just as I get my pint, a mere six minutes into the match. We're playing calm, possession football and a great fourteen-man passing move sees the ball reach Victor Moses on the edge of the box. He's given too much space and fizzes a low drive into the corner of City's net. Maybe Hart should have done a little better, but still a great strike from Victor. So it looks like the usual routine win at a top-five side, though City go close as Agüero rounds Adrián, but thankfully shoots wide.

Meanwhile, I'm receiving text updates from the Wellington

pub, where train robber Buster Edwards used to drink. Matt, Lisa, Fraser, Gavin and Michael are gathered hoping to see West Ham pull off a similar heist. After half an hour we gain a corner, with City claiming, incorrectly, that the ball hadn't fully crossed the line. Reid wins a header, Obiang does well to keep the ball alive and it rebounds to Sakho, who prods home from close range. OMG. This cannot be happening. We nearly make it three when a superb tackle from Mangala denies Sakho in the box.

Her Indoors has booked us tickets that night for a 7.30 p.m. performance of *Lady Anna All at Sea* at the Park Theatre. Matt texts to ask if I'll be able to see the end of the game. I reply that 'I might have to leave a few minutes before the whistle when the score is the usual 3-0.'

All West Ham need to do is not concede before half-time. Only we've reckoned without Agüero finding De Bruyne on the edge of the area and the £55 million signing powering a low shot home. Matt texts to say that my overconfident words have jinxed us. Though he's forgetting that this is a new West Ham, where the old rules don't apply.

For the second half, I move to the World's End pub closer to the Park Theatre and endure a long, long forty-five minutes as City play well and dominate. But Winston Reid is absolutely immense, winning numerous tackles and making more clearances than any other Premier League defender so far this season. Winston will never surrender. Bilić and the new signings have improved the side, but let's also credit Sam Allardyce for the improvement in Reid; he looked a liability under Avram Grant, but Allardyce saw his potential and helped him became the player he is today.

Adrián has an inspired game in goal and the pick of his saves are a one-on-one with Agüero and a tip over the bar from Otamendi's header. Tomkins isn't far behind in heroics and Jenkinson bravely lunges into tackles even though he's been injured. City are a bit unlucky, too, when Touré's shot goes just past the post. West Ham create a couple of rare chances, with Payet finding Sakho, who fires wide, and Jelavić almost connects late on.

In the dying minutes, Payet has a long-range effort saved, but it's then relentless City pressure at the Council House. I have to leave two minutes into added time to get to the theatre, knowing that City will surely equalise – just as everyone else scored against us in added time last season – but I'm telling myself that a point will still be a good result. As I take my seat in the gallery, phone illicitly in hand, the incredible news comes through on BBC Sport that we've held out.

Never in doubt! You wait decades for wins at Arsenal, Liverpool and Man City and then three come along at once. And it's only September. If only I'd had a bet… 'This can't be happening…' texts my old school pal Mark. We go second! What a start, what a season so far.

Even losing away to Leicester in the League Cup the following Tuesday can't dampen my elation. We at least take them to extra time before King's headed winner. Zárate comes in and scores a deflected goal. So we'll just have to win the FA Cup now.

Meanwhile I find myself doing a hasty photoshoot outside the gates at the Boleyn Ground that Thursday evening as *The Guardian* is publishing my piece on my family memories of Upton Park. My elder daughter Lola is having to miss a geography lecture at the Royal Geographical Society, while fourteen-year-old Nell is behind with her homework and I'm consumed by bad parent/good fan dilemmas.

Despite the rain and dusky light, photographer Graham Turner does a fine job persuading us to pose with a variety of hats, scarves and flags. Our football history has been strangely intertwined with the Family section of *The Guardian*. They took a picture of my daughter Lola and me at her first game by Belly Busters burger bar and of my dad and me at his final game by these very gates.

These Boleyn Ground gates involve a lot of memories; my Dad and I used to trek through them and veer to the left to the North Bank turnstiles and join the OAPs and boys' queue. Inside the North Bank was the promise of Bovril and roasted peanuts… And few could forget the hundreds of shirts and memorials laid out on the railings after Bobby Moore died in 1993, or the poignant messages left by fans. I remember one said simply, 'Heaven has a new captain.' After his death we suddenly realised how both the club and the football establishment had neglected Bobby.

Photoshoot and intimations of mortality over, the girls and I head home via the Queens Fish Bar next to the station.

The following Saturday sees West Ham at home to Norwich City. My piece is in *The Guardian*, which gives a glow to the day as I buy my programme at the Tube. Today's issue has a cover in the style of the 1971/72 season, which immediately evokes memories of illicit pints of beer with my dad in the Moby Dick off the North Circular on the way home after evening matches. And of that superb advert on the back of *Hammer* with a full-page picture of Billy Bonds in an open-necked '70s shirt, complete with hairy chest, sideburns and medallion and generally looking like he should be in *Life on Mars*. The advertising copy read: 'There are only two things that never let you down, whatever the conditions, week in week out, season after season, especially when the going gets tough. The other's a Ford from Reynolds.'

But back to reality in 2015...

Looking at my piece in *The Guardian* online that morning it's certainly generated a lot of comments. They're mainly positive, including one succinct summary from Jamie, whose first game was a Cup Winners' Cup quarter-final against Lausanne in 1965: 'It was a dump, but what an atmosphere.' A couple of other fans reminisce about the 8-1 victory over Newcastle in 1986, when Peter Beardsley had to go in goal for the Geordies. A fan now in Namibia recalls his first game, a 4-0 win over Blackpool in 1966.

A woman whose East End family were shipped out to South Harrow writes:

> I went often to Upton Park during the dark days of the 1980s – when being a female on the terraces was a rare thing and conventional wisdom had it that only fighting drunkards went to football anyway – as well as to away matches to stadia long gone (Roker Park, Ayresome Park, the Baseball Ground, Underhill, Highbury...). So sorry that Boleyn is to be added to that list – but it's been fifteen years since I went to see a Premiership/League match. I was evidently one of those fans that clubs were keen to be rid of: a working-class, stand-there-in-all-weathers, smoking, flask-of-Bovril-smuggling fan who'd started going as a small child in the early 1970s

> – but who couldn't pay for a £wtf season ticket nor even a match ticket most days.

Several comments come from supporters of other clubs. Everton fan Jon remembers: 'Always enjoyed watching Everton play at West 'Aaam, a proper bearpit of a ground, raucous and intimidating.' A Middlesbrough fans recalls the uncivil reception he received from the ICF back in the days when it was 'a dangerous hell hole of a ground', while West Brom fan Kismet comments:

> Have ace memories of West Brom at Upton Park in the '80s. Classic fun times. Particularly, our lads wearing WHU badges so they could walk around the ground unmolested. Once at the bar, and as a direct consequence of the acid they were on, they then started claiming there are West Ham in here and staring at all and sundry including each other. At some point I was one of six Albion for a Full Members Cup defeat. We almost got the car towed as we'd parked in the director's bay, and were then outed as Albion in the home seats and it managed to become moody. With six. On a Wednesday. In the Full Members Cup.

There's surely a whole book to be filled with bad acid trips at Upton Park…

And so it's on to Ken's Café. It's the week of 'piggate', the Twitter-inspired controversy that blew up following the serialisation of *Call Me Dave*, a new book on David Cameron that has some lurid tales of the PM's Bullingdon Club antics at Oxford University. Inside Ken's, our team of Matt, Lisa, Michael and Nigel is discussing initiation ceremonies at drinking societies. 'I joined the BullingDon Hutchison Society,' quips Matt, referring to West Ham's one-time midfielder 'Deadly' Don Hutchison.

We're joined by Matt's brother Adam, who's over from Melbourne. Later that evening, Adam's mates in his home town of Basingstoke are putting on a special geezerpunk gig for him, so surely the Irons will also do their bit for a man who's travelled 12,000 miles. Though maybe not, as Nigel starts saying that we'll be top if we win and Man City lose, causing groans from all sides of the brown-sauce-strewn table, as we're always alert to portents that might offend the footballing deities.

Meanwhile, Michael the Whovian is carrying a mysterious West Ham bag, which contains the costume he plans to wear to the evening's performance of *The Rocky Horror Show*. He won't show us its contents. The stewards' search outside the East Stand should be interesting.

There's a decent atmosphere as the game kicks off. 'We're Norwich City, we'll sing on our own!' chant the away fans, only to be met with a chant of 'You're shagging your sister!' from the Bobby Moore Stand.

West Ham look positive for the opening nine minutes, until Mark Noble tries to find James Tomkins with a cross-field pass. Robbie Brady nicks the ball and scores. Norwich gain in confidence and look like adding a second as Jerome fires into the side netting. The Irons appear tired after playing extra time at Leicester.

'Losing at home to a newly promoted side – it feels like we're doing the Time Warp again,' I suggest to Michael.

'Our defence is certainly rocky and it's a bit of a horror show,' he concurs.

Even Payet is misplacing passes, but suddenly we equalise. Sakho finds Payet out on the right and the Reunion magician races down the flank to send in a low cross that is met by Sakho's well-timed run. It's a tap-in for Diafra (not 'Biafra', as the programme called him).

Lanzini has a free kick just wide, but it's 1-1 at the interval. The second half sees more Norwich chances as Adrián flies to his top corner like Superman to tip over Howson's effort.

Fowl! There's a bizarre stoppage as an injured pigeon lands on the turf. Making the catch of the day, to quote the tabloids, the Canaries' Jonny Howson picks it up and removes it to the touchline to big cheers – though one fan suggests it's going straight into one of Delia Smith's pies.

'Julian Dicks would just have stamped on it!' offers someone behind us.

Post-pigeon, the game continues. Victor Moses sends in a great cross from the right and Sakho gets a firm header at goal, but it's too close to Ruddy, who makes a fine stop. Sakho runs at the City defence and, surrounded by four men, he does really well to pick out Payet, who cuts inside a defender and is denied by a good Ruddy save. In turn, City's Howson pulls the ball back for Jerome, who looks certain to score, only for Adrián to save with his face, which stuns the keeper. He eventually recovers and earns his applause.

Andy Carroll comes on and within a minute goes down after stretching for the ball. The whole stadium is united in trepidation, fearing yet another injury. You can hear the collective gasp. But thankfully Andy gets up and plays on.

It's Norwich who look likely to win as Brady's free kick is tipped round the post by Adrián. The corner is cleared, but the ball returns to sub Redmond, who cuts inside Mark Noble too easily and fires into the corner at the Trevor Brooking Stand end. Seven minutes to go. Looks like we've now lost to two newly promoted teams at home.

We revert to lumping the ball towards Big Andy up front and on ninety minutes he almost takes the ball past the keeper, only to be foiled by a good catch by Ruddy. It's always other teams that score against us in added time, never us.

We're in the third minute of added time when Reid is fouled on the right. Payet plays in a hopeful free kick. Ruddy is so concerned by the presence of Carroll that he punches the ball weakly. It rebounds off Big Andy and falls to Kouyaté, who fires home. The Bobby Moore Stand is a writhing mass of fist-pumping arms. Kouyaté runs into the arms of the gleeful fans in the corner as he celebrates. Phew. Feels like a win now. Credit to Carroll for being a big lump and scaring the Norwich defence.

As 'If the Kids Are United' and 'Teenage Kicks' reverberate from the PA, we retreat to the Central. It was important we got something out of the game today and, looking at my glass half-full of Old Speckled Hen, we're unbeaten in four league matches and still third. Matt's brother Adam looks relieved to be returning to Australia with a point. It was a tired-looking performance, but there's no denying the spirit of the side. And hopefully that pigeon will soon be flying so high and nearly reaching the sky, if Delia's not nabbed it that is.

As October begins, West Ham face lowly Sunderland away. The sort of game we used to lose and a real test of the Irons' newfound solidity away from home. Listening to the Radio London commentary, West Ham are lucky not to be four down at half-time.

Sunderland gaffer Dick Advocaat is rumoured to be on the verge of quitting but a suddenly rejuvenated Sunderland team seem to be trying to persuade him to stay. Fletcher scores from a training ground free-kick routine and then Lens doubles the tally with a superb chip over Adrián. The Irons' custodian makes a great save from O'Shea and Borini misses a couple of good chances. But suddenly there's hope. Right on half-time Carl Jenkinson strokes the ball home after good work by Moses on the left wing. It's the right-back's first goal for the Hammers.

Winless Sunderland are increasingly nervous in the second half. When Lens is red-carded, the home side become even more desperate. The equaliser arrives when Lanzini's long-distance shot is parried by Pantilimon and Dimitri Payet scores from the rebound for his fourth of the season. The last half an hour sees a lot of West Ham corners and sub Jelavić scoops over from a yard out. In a way it's two points lost as the last half-hour is all West Ham, but we lack a quality final ball. Still, after being battered in the first half, I'm grateful for a point. Unbeaten on the road and seventeen goals so far this season– it's certainly not been dull.

⚽ ⚽ ⚽

The next Saturday it's off to London Bridge to meet Matt and Lisa for our trip to Norwood Junction and Crystal Palace versus West Ham. Matt and Lisa's choice of pre-match nosh comes from a website of posh cafés near football grounds, so we head to Coffee Craft located in the Victorian, Grade II-listed Stanley Halls in Norwood. The portraits, armchairs and bone china can't quite match Kenneth's Café in Green Street, though the flat white coffee, hummus and pitta, cheese and tomato paninis and butterfly cakes almost surpass Carol's egg, chips and beans.

Inside the concourse of the Arthur Wait Stand there are hearty choruses of 'One man and his dog couldn't carry Lampard!' Then we watch the pre-match eagle handler and the Crystals feeling 'Glad All Over'. Pleasingly, Palace have splashed out on plastic seats to replace the ancient wooden artefacts we sat on last season.

West Ham attack from the kick-off. Noble finds Lanzini with a fine ball to the left wing and Manuel's dribble to the by-line sees Payet scuff what should be the opening goal. Encouraged by this, the West Ham fans break into a chorus of 'My name is Luděk Mikloško, I come from near Moscow...' There's also a new song about Dimitri Payet being Super Slaven's man and better than Zidane. Matt – whom I never had down as a country fan – identifies it as being sung to the tune of Billy Ray Cyrus's 1992 theme song 'Achy Breaky Heart'.

Yes, that's Billy Ray, Miley Cyrus's dad, who sported a very unfortunate mullet back in '92. Billy Ray's adapted lyrics are now being hollered by geezers in claret-and-blue. The new song goes: 'We've got Payet, Dimitri Payet! I just don't think you understand. He's Super Slav's man, he's better than Zidane. We've got Dimitri Payet!'

West Ham fans have not previously been known for sporting Billy Ray Cyrus-style mullets or a love of country music, but do have form on the dodgy tunes front, having once changed Spandau Ballet's 'Gold' to 'Always believe in Carlton Cole!'

Still, it's very memorable and suits Payet. Rather appropriately, bearing in mind the Miley Cyrus connection, West Ham start to take a wrecking ball to Crystal Palace. Perhaps Billy Ray and Miley might join President Obama – who once went to a match at Upton Park – among the United States' celebrity Hammers fans. Though whether Miley, or indeed dad Billy, would ever perform in a West Ham shirt, as Katy Perry once did when married to Russell Brand, is still uncertain.

Lanzini looks bright in midfield and we're playing some nice passing football. West Ham take the lead on twenty-two minutes. Payet cuts inside to find Victor Moses, who plays a perfect through-ball to Jenkinson, who has ghosted past the sleeping Zaha. Carl finishes like Michael Owen (at least according to Garth Crooks) for his second goal in successive games. We're splashed with beer and jumping blokes as Jenks runs towards us.

In the ensuing goal celebration, Lisa suffers a celebratory injury as her glasses are bumped and cut her nose. She's shed blood for the claret-and-blue cause. Just as we're wondering why Mark Clattenburg hasn't stopped play for Lisa to receive treatment, the ball goes down the other end and Jenkinson upends Gayle. The penalty has to be taken twice due to encroachment in the area, but Cabaye scores both times. The Palace Ultras start to chant their silly song.

West Ham are offered more hope of a win shortly before the break when Clattenburg books Gayle for a second time after his lunge on Kouyaté. Still, it's always difficult to play against ten men, particularly if you're West Ham.

The second half sees solid West Ham pressure as Palace sit back with two banks of four. Sakho sends a header against the outside of a post. Palace still have the pace of Sako and Bolasie up front and the returning James Collins has an excellent game, repeatedly nicking the ball off the Palace strikers. When he goes down after taking a football in the goolies, but recovers to make a great tackle, he earns a worthy chorus of 'One Ginger Pelé! There's only one Ginger Pelé!'

A lot of West Ham passes from Kouyaté and Noble go astray though and even Payet plays his share of bad balls as we struggle to get through. A wonderful dribble from Lanzini ends when he is tackled in the box. On come Big Andy Carroll, Zárate and Jelavić.

Carroll has one decent shot over the bar but often drifts too far back to receive the ball, while Zárate shoots ineffectually wide. Mystic Matt suggests we should take the tiring Lanzini off. It looks like the game is drifting towards a draw until the eighty-eighth minute. Zárate at last manages to get in an excellent cross, Andy Carroll heads back across the box, Jelavić and a defender scuffle for and miss the ball, but Lanzini arrives to shoot home. The young Argentine midfielder deserves the goal and more mayhem ensues in the Arthur Wait Stand. Bringing Carroll on from a very strong bench has changed the game.

Can we hold on? There's one more tackle from Collins to thwart Bolasie and, with four minutes of added time played, West Ham break again. Lanzini plays another great ball through to Dimitri Payet who casually chips the ball over Hennessey. He has more class than the average edition of *Country Life*. The French wizard then runs to the corner flag to deliver a military salute to the Palace fans, who are now feeling bad all over. Is he the best player we've seen since Di Canio?

'Another twenty-three points and we're safe!' suggests someone on the very slow 'fast' train back to London Bridge. Matt's even had some Twitter banter going with Palace-supporting comedian Mark Steel. We retreat to the Old Eagle in Camden Town, where we enjoy pints of Betty Stogs Cornish ale before I attend Martha's gig, in aid of my pal Adam's late daughter, at Camden Girls' School. In the Old Eagle there are candles on the table and Lisa sits in front of a portrait of the Mona Lisa – it's almost like being in the Central.

Over our beers we reflect that one of the notable features of the win at Palace is the amount of talent on the West Ham bench. Our subs were Andy Carroll, Nikica Jelavić, Mauro Zárate, Enner Valencia, Pedro Obiang, Angelo Ogbonna and Darren Randolph. That's some £50 million worth of talent, while £7 million Michail Antonio couldn't even make the bench. The fact that Bilić used Carroll, Jelavić and Zárate to offer something different up front certainly helped end the resistance of Palace's ten men after the starting eleven ran out of ideas.

It was only a few weeks ago that we had six kids on the bench at Anfield in Lee, Oxford, Cullen, Samuelson, Knoyle and Spiegel. The seven who made it to the bench at Palace are surely the strongest set of subs in West Ham's history.

A good away day for the travelling Irons. We've stayed patient and for once managed to beat a team that's down to ten men. We go fourth. Unbeaten away from home in five games now; this is heady stuff.

5

IN KEN'S CAFÉ WE TRUST

KEN'S CAFÉ IS A PRE-MATCH INSTITUTION AT WEST HAM. On match days the queues stretch through the door and out into Green Street. Ken's son Gary sells burgers on a stall outside while there's a solitary pavement table and two chairs for that Paris-meets-E13 sensation. Ken's is only the size of a normal two-up, two-down Green Street house, but it fits in a tremendous number of customers. Instead of an overpriced stadium pie or hot dog, you can still get egg, chips and beans with two slices of toast and a cup of tea for less than a fiver.

Wooden chairs sit alongside the sides of each table and your back is tight against the other customers. To leave often entails having to get the entire row to stand up. Staff jostle through the queue holding plates of fry-ups and sausage sandwiches, saying, 'Mind yer backs!' Or they shout 'Forty-eight! I ain't telling yer again! Who's got forty-eight?' before dispensing plates and cutlery to dozy customers who suddenly realise their number is up.

The tables are topped with blue Formica and have plastic bottles of ketchup and brown sauce along with a sugar dispenser and salt and pepper pots. A TV is mounted on a bracket beneath the ceiling, dispensing daytime drama. Hand-written menus on orange card adorn the walls, offering various combinations of sausage, egg, chips, beans and bacon, plus toasted sandwiches and a big breakfast with black pudding, liver, bacon, mash and peas.

Also on the walls are pictures of West Ham's 1980 FA Cup-winning side, a photo of Billy Bonds holding a baby and a set of pictures of 1960s icons Bobby Moore, Geoff Hurst, Martin Peters, Frank Lampard, Harry Redknapp, Billy Bonds, Bobby Ferguson, Clive Charles and Alan Stephenson. Also making the cut is a picture of some laughing policemen, a West Ham bulldog, a West Ham mirror and a set of mounted guns on either side of the café.

Behind the counter is Carol, in her blue apron, dispensing tea you can stand your spoon up in from an urn and numbered tickets for each food order. To her left is a glass shelf containing Swiss rolls, fruitcake, Kit-Kats and Twixes. She'll admonish customers who have bought their programme outside and not from her box on the counter, share a joke and shout for someone to get more cups. Hundreds of fans all get fed on time. She's the best manager West Ham never had.

Ken and Carol Lucas have plenty of stories to tell. Ken emerges from his kitchen to make a rare appearance in the café itself and makes himself a coffee, joining Carol and myself at a table. Did they ever used to get any footballers in?

'Frank Lampard Senior used to have a business two doors away and he'd sneak in for his sausage sandwich with masses of brown sauce,' remembers Carol.

'I put a load of brown sauce on it,' adds Ken, who cooks all the food in the kitchen at the back of the café aided by his daughter Sarah Jane. 'But he said, "It ain't enough." I said, "Just have the bottle!"'

'We had half the team in here – Bobby Moore, Geoff Hurst … a lot of the youngsters come in the old days. But they're prima donnas now aren't they, with their tinted windows, not signing autographs like in the old days,' says Carol. Though Carlton Cole did come in more recently. 'It made my grandson Billy's day and though he wasn't meant to eat it, Carlton mullered his bacon sandwich!'

The good news is that the café is staying open next season

after the Irons move to Stratford. 'No, we are not closing down!' emphasises Carol. 'We'll just potter along, as long as we get to the end of the week with enough to cover us.'

Ken, who recently turned eighty, owns the café outright, so fans will still be able to get their pre-match grub in Green Street before taking a bus or taxi to Stratford.

Carol is legendary for her front-of-house skills at the cash desk, dispensing tickets, organising her team of staff (including three generations of her family) and generally keeping the fans in order and the meals arriving within twenty minutes.

Carol, who is a few years younger than Ken but never seems to age, was originally from Slough, and Ken from Streatham. They met at the Southend Kursaal when Carol was on the coach and Ken was riding his motorbike. After accepting a ride home on Ken's bike, Carol was in trouble with her parents, but romance quickly blossomed.

Having been a cook in the army, Ken was working as a lorry driver, but fancied opening a café. In 1967, two years after marrying Carol, he looked over No. 467 Green Street. 'I parked my lorry outside. The law come in and said, "You've got to move your lorry, there's a match on in two hours." I didn't even know West Ham was here!' recalls Ken.

When Ken and Carol took over the premises it was an amusement arcade. They still live upstairs and four of their children were born there. Ken kept a few machines in the café, though this led to problems with, what he terms, 'a few Herberts from Canning Town'.

'We had all the rockers in here and all the mods went to a place in Plaistow,' remembers Carol. 'I told them we can't have German helmets in here, it's a Jewish area!'

'One of them came in with a shotgun. I said, "I'm not having that in here!"' laughs Ken. 'You see 'em now and they're all granddads. When I say "Do you remember the shotgun?", they go, "Sshhh!"'

Back in the 1960s and 1970s, Ken's Café did an unlikely trade selling bacon sandwiches to Rabbis from the nearby synagogue. 'It was a very Jewish area when we moved here,' says Carol. 'The market was mainly Jewish and next door was a Jewish lady selling materials. The rabbis would sneak in, and him next door, every time his wife went to the warehouse, he'd say, "Quick, Ken, get me a sandwich!"'

But it was the football trade that really helped the café prosper. Ken and Carol are proud of the fact that customers on match days are usually served within twenty minutes and nothing is cooked until it's ordered. 'Keep the fat hot!' is Ken's sage advice for feeding industrial quantities of chips to hungry fans.

They've had the odd mishap, though, such as the time a fryer broke down and, 'the time the electric went off, so we did it by candlelight – but we still fed 'em!'

Ken and Carol are happy to serve fans of any hue, though if there's any aggravation it's normally Carol who sorts it out. 'I can shout them out, because they're not likely to hit a woman,' explains Carol. 'But the worst football fan was a woman in her eighties, quiet as a mouse. Then one person came in wearing another team's colours and she was like a volcano. The most she ever managed was three games before we threw her out again.'

Even the police used to like a secret cuppa round the back. 'In came one of the chiefs saying, "Have you got any of my officers in there?" I said "no", but we had eight of them in the scullery at the back!' laughs Carol.

Over the years, the café's displays of replica guns on the walls have caused some talking points. 'This girl said, "Are them guns real?" I said, "Yes, the only thing you've got to do is don't slam the door when you leave." She flew out of here!' chuckles Ken. 'The law came in and he said, "I've got to have you about these guns", until I told him they were plastic. We did have one of them nicked once and about a month later the bank was robbed!'

Ken's Café has had its share of well-known customers, such as *Never Mind the Buzzcocks*' Phill Jupitus and Ken Livingstone when he was running for mayor. 'Ken's alright, though I don't like his politics. He saw the sign at the front and said, "My café!" We've had *EastEnders* stars too –

I'm dreadful for names, I just see faces,' says Carol. 'What I like is the celebrities that are just like any other punter. They queue up, they don't expect special treatment. They're not here as celebrities, they just want to be one of the punters. So I won't let anyone molest them.'

Other memorable moments at Ken's include a car swerving in Green Street and coming through the front window some ten years ago. 'I was sitting here doing my books and, crash, a car come in. The whole side of the shop come down. I got a new front out of him though,' says Ken. The café has also had a window smashed by an irate window cleaner (he had a grudge against the previous owner) and it was once burnt down – but only on celluloid, when it was used as a film set.

Thanks to their match-day regulars, Ken and Carol have been recognised in unusual places. Ken recalls: 'We were at Center Parcs in Nottingham and this big bunch of Herberts came over. I said "watch it" but as they got nearer they said "Ken's Café!! How are yer?!" What a relief! We were at the Isle of Wight in a chip shop late at night and the guy says, "I've seen you before in Ken's Café!"'

There was talk at one point of a committee being formed to help local businesses move to Stratford, but the pair say no more was heard of that. They remain sceptical about West Ham's move to Stratford and Carol bemoans the flat prices of the planned development of the Boleyn Ground. 'It's rock bottom for housing in this borough, you can get five families in one house, and there should be more social housing.'

Football provides a link for fans with an old industrial East End that's gone, and in its way so too does Ken's Café, representing an East End that's disappeared, or at least moved out to Essex. Much of Green Street is curry houses and samosas now, and although it's a fine place to eat, it's still fantastic to find a genuine old 1960s-style East End café. Once, in the days when Italian and Chinese and Indian restaurants seemed incredibly exotic, caffs were the closest working-class people ever came to eating out.

Ken's Café today is pretty much the same as it's always been and that's part of its charm and why authentic cafés are back in fashion. Ken and Carol do seem genuinely happy in their work and will carry on. It's a proper caff and they're a London culinary treasure.

'They won't give us that fifth star for food because they want lighting and marble floors and posh chairs and a toilet,' says Carol. 'People are fed up with Costa Coffee and all this espresso double this, double that. But we won't change!' And none of their customers would ever want them to.

6

STICK YOUR BLUE FLAG UP YOUR…

CHELSEA ARE THE NEXT VISITORS UPTON PARK, WITH manager José Mourinho an increasingly strange, paranoid figure as his Blues continue to underachieve. Tabloid rumours suggest he's not long for the job.

My first stop on match day is the Newham Bookshop in Barking Road. Vivian has lined up Danny Dyer for a signing, she reveals as I peruse signed copies of Elvis Costello's new book *Unfaithful Music and Disappearing Ink*, complete with valuable advice for today's game in his song title 'I Don't Want to Go to Chelsea'.

Then it's on to Ken's Café, where condensation sits on the windows and the smell of frying pervades the air. There's much debate about who bought a ceramic model of Ken's Café from the V&A for £150 and Carol behind the counter says she'd like to get hold of it for Ken's birthday. Charles Saatchi will just have to give it up.

Lisa has been to the Victoria and Albert Museum's Tower of Babel exhibition by artist Barnaby Barford and discovered that it featured china models of both Ken's Café and the Newham Bookshop. The blurb describes the six-metre-tall tower, made up of 3,000 china buildings, as 'Barnaby Barford's representation of London today.' Nice to have definitive proof that Ken's Café is of huge artistic and architectural merit.

Meanwhile, Michael the Whovian has been to see Jo Grant, aka Katy Manning from *Doctor Who*, in *Nobody's Business* at the King's Head Theatre in Islington. There's even a fleeting appearance from Northern Ireland-born Iron DC with his 'wee men', telling us all to cut down on the sugar and processed meat.

We take the usual route down Tudor Road and along the alleyway by the old bus station, before Nigel and Matt steam in by the away coaches and recycle their papers in Newham Council's wheelie bins.

The game kicks off with rousing versions of 'Bubbles', 'Stick your blue flag up your arse!' and a certain song about John Terry's mum. It's good to have a proper old-time atmosphere inside Upton Park.

Payet wins a free kick on the edge of the box after sixteen minutes. The French magician takes it himself and Begović tips it over the bar. From Payet's corner Costa slices across goal and Zárate sends a crisp, first-time shot into the bottom corner. Upton Park explodes. It's vindication of Bilić's decision to pick Zárate in place of the ineligible Moses. That's Zárate's fourth goal of the season and credit to Bilić for finally rejuvenating his career.

The way Bilić has handled Zárate has been impressive. Mauro fell out with Big Sam after being dropped last season and was loaned out to QPR, only for Rangers gaffer Harry Redknapp to try to swap him for Matt Jarvis. After Redknapp resigned, Mauro had more problems with Rangers' new boss Chris Ramsey and was fined for his reaction after being omitted against Liverpool. Back then it looked like he had no future at West Ham.

Earlier in the season, Bilić fined winger Morgan Amalfitano for 'a breach of rules' and had him training with the kids before he was eventually released. It proved that Slaven was definitely in charge. Yet, he's also handled Zárate sensitively. We've had no strops even when he's been out of the side and Slaven finally seems to be getting the best out of him. And with Payet, Lanzini and Zárate, we now have three number ten-type players who can turn a game.

Zárate's goal pleases the home fans no end. Mourinho is

taunted with 'Sacked in the morning… You're getting sacked in the morning!' and even the East Stand joins in. Then it's 'That's why you're going down!'

West Ham should make it two when an outrageous back-heel from Payet plays in Lanzini, who chips it over the bar. Matić is booked for a professional foul on the rampaging Cheikhou Kouyaté, but then Chelsea come back into it. Zouma has a header cleared from behind the line by Lanzini (technology proves the ball wasn't completely over the line) and then Chelsea break from a West Ham corner. Fabregas nets, but he's ruled marginally offside by a knee and shoulder. José doesn't look happy.

Matić then receives a second yellow for pulling back Sakho and is dismissed to huge cheers and much waving goodbye from the home fans. Fabregas and Terry are booked for protesting. Chelsea lose any semblance of discipline as coach Silvino Louro is dismissed by referee Jonathan Moss (a better ref than Culture Club drummer, suggests Matt) just before the break. Initially the crowd believes it's Mourinho who's gone.

But we learn from social media that at half-time Mourinho has also been dismissed for visiting the referee's room and swearing at him. 'F**k off, Mourinho!' is the verdict of the Bobby Moore Stand, who haven't as yet come up with a chant featuring *Schadenfreude*.

'One-nil up against ten men with no manager. What could possibly go wrong?' I quip to Nigel as he munches on his lucky half-time banana.

Ominously, ten-man Chelsea improve after the break. Cahill equalises, turning quickly on a loose ball from a corner. They are still the Champions, after all. At this stage Chelsea look the likelier winners and we'd take the point. But Bilić rejigs things by bringing on Big Andy Carroll for Zárate with twenty-one minutes to go. Payet raises hopes with a couple of brilliant feints and then some great showboating as he flicks the ball over the head of a defender, only to shoot wide. Show a bit of audacity and the crowd here will love you.

Sakho has worked immensely hard, as always, and closes down Begović to force a corner with eleven minutes left. Payet's cross is hoofed up in the air by a defender and the ball comes to Cresswell. The left-back sends in a superb cross and Andy Carroll rises above Sakho and Cahill like a Geordie version of the Shard to power home a header. In that position he's unstoppable. Andy races towards our corner to slide onto the turf and is engulfed by his teammates. They'll be dancing in the streets of Brentwood tonight. He leaves two great tyre tracks in the grass from his slide. Had he not slowed down, he might easily have demolished part of the East Stand.

There's a hugely celebratory mood now as the Bobby Moore Stand bounces up and down to 'Up your arse, up your arse! From Stamford Bridge to Upton Park, we'll stick your blue flag up your arse!' Then it's 'We've got Payet, Dimitri Payet, I just don't think you understand...' Though Billy Ray Cyrus expert Fraser says they haven't got the tempo of 'Achy Breaky Heart' quite right.

We were all optimistic last season after beating Liverpool and Man City early on, but the thought occurs that perhaps this West Ham side is on the verge of something special. And it's also poignant that this is the last time we'll ever tell Chelsea where to place their blue flag at the Boleyn.

There's four minutes of added time and with a minute to go I have to make a dash for the Tube to try to get the 5.45 p.m. train to Cardiff for a wedding reception (who gets married on a football day, eh?). There's a chorus of 'We can see you sneaking out!' from the lads, but the huge cheer from the stadium as I leave the East Stand tells its own story.

I don't make the 5.45 p.m. train as there's a long halt due to 'a passenger being taken ill at Farringdon'. 'It must be Mourinho!' suggests a fellow passenger. Matt texts that the Central have got their tactics all wrong by having no staff, a bit like Chelsea, while I celebrate on the 6.45 p.m. train with a pint of London Porter purchased from M&S at Paddington.

Arsenal, Liverpool, Man City and now Chelsea. A great

day for the Hammers. Though I still think Chelsea are too good to go down… My euphoria is sustained all the way to Cardiff. Nicola and my daughters are already at Raoul and Julian's wedding reception as I take a taxi and arrive at some Doric-columned venue near the university. 'We won! And José Mourinho was sent off!' I tell my family, before searching through the remnants of food and beer as Abba comes on the disco.

The following Tuesday, Chelsea are charged by the FA with behaving like toddlers. Though I'm not sure why West Ham are also charged with failing to control their players, unless it's to prevent another Mourinho tirade. Chelsea appear to have lost all sense of discipline. They had six players booked, a coach sent off and their manager sent to the stands after entering the referee's room at half-time. Then Mourinho refused to give a TV interview after the game, despite being obliged to do so, and left poor Gary Cahill to speak to the press. Despite looking a little embarrassed, Cahill made a decent job of it and didn't whinge like his manager.

You'd like to think West Ham learned a little about how to lose with good grace in the days of Ron Greenwood and John Lyall, and what was striking about Chelsea's attitude was a complete lack of sporting behaviour. Matić deserved his two yellow cards; Zouma's header was nearly over the line but not quite and the goal-line technology proved it; while Fabregas's goal was a close call, but he was offside by an elbow. Some refs would have allowed it, others wouldn't. And Adrián had already stopped moving having heard the whistle. No huge conspiracy there, yet José Mourinho continues to talk himself out of a job. He deserved to be sent to the stands and taunted by Danny Dyer, who was filmed on YouTube quipping, 'Alright, sunshine?' to the Napoleonic One, before being ushered away by a steward.

West Ham fans are traditionally wary of jinxes. The Monday after the game I bump into my near-neighbour Nick, also a Hammers fan, who jokes, 'Just so long as Andy Carroll doesn't start saying we'll finish in the top four, we'll have grounds for optimism.' As soon as Andy said West Ham wanted to win the league last season, we slumped and only won three games after Christmas.

Andy has kept quiet so far this season, but it's a little worrying that after Chelsea win co-chairman David Sullivan appears on West Ham TV daring to dream, saying, 'Us or maybe Leicester could break into the top four this year... I know it's unlikely but it is possible.' As we all know in the East Stand, never predict the score, never check the league table until the final whistle and always wear your lucky shirt.

Predictably we then get hammered at Watford in a Halloween horror show. At least Bilić is honest in his appraisal that West Ham were complacent and the performance was unacceptable, with WHU second-best from the start. James Collins getting red-carded rounds off a bad day. Sub Enner Valencia does at least hit a post for the Hammers. Watching it on *Match of the Day*, Carroll dawdles horribly in his own box for the first goal and Tomkins should have cut out the cross for Ighalo's second, while Collins's red card is a stupid tackle probably coming out of frustration at West Ham's poor performance.

West Ham have failed to beat all the newly promoted teams, taking just one point from Bournemouth, Norwich and Watford. Watford are clearly a well-organised unit with an in-form striker, but it's worrying we should have fallen into the old trap of playing well against the big boys and slumping against the lesser teams. Bilić still has work to do...

Perhaps Watford was a one-off. Just as long as we can keep Payet fit we can still have a great season. Heavy rain saturates Green Street on an unseasonably humid day as I arrive at Ken's Café clad in my Gore-Tex for the visit of Everton on 5 November. Matt and Nigel are discussing old horror films as Matt becomes possibly the first person ever to utter the word 'portmanteau' in Ken's. Meanwhile, Michael the Renaissance Man (and Whovian) maintains a Zen-like calm, insisting that his big breakfast will arrive before kick-off, despite the fact he's arrived at 2.15 p.m.

Carol's granddaughter is the latest family member to have been recruited on cup-collecting duties, while Carol herself is still trying to trace the person who bought the pottery model of Ken's Café from the V&A exhibition by Barnaby Barford. There's time for late appearances from my Facebook pal Nicola, Phill Jupitus and Big Joe and then a dash to the East Stand, with Matt and Nigel making their obligatory trek to the recycling bins.

We arrive to find squaddies in West Ham scarves on the pitch, a minute's silence for Remembrance Day and 'The Last Post' being played. Winston Reid's in for the suspended Collins and Sakho is still injured so Andy Carroll starts two successive games for the first time since January.

The sides appear pretty evenly matched, but West Ham make a decent start. Everton are unexpectedly physical and Koné clatters Moses without being booked. Another fine ball from Payet finds Jenkinson, who shoots at the keeper rather than crossing. Michael, never slow to miss a Christian allegory, wonders if Moses will deliver his commandments on tablets of Stones. The Everton centre-back is impressive throughout, dominating Andy Carroll, and earns a tuneful cover of the Beatles' hit 'Money Can't Buy Me Stones' from the away fans.

The Irons take the lead after half an hour. Payet finds the impressive Moses, who scuffs his shot from the edge of the box. The ball rebounds off Stones to Lanzini on the edge of the box and he curls a lovely effort into the top corner before running into the corner to celebrate.

Payet has already delighted the crowd with one pirouette away from Everton's midfield on the halfway line, provoking a chorus of 'We've got Payet!', but is crocked by McCarthy with a dangerous scissor tackle. The Everton enforcer plays a bit of the ball, but also clatters the man from behind with his trailing leg. It could easily be a straight red card, but ref Paul Tierney only books him. Matt is tempted to start a McCarthyite witch-hunt. Payet is down for aeons and there's a collective intake of breath before he picks himself up.

Two minutes before the break, Everton equalise, just after the PA announces, 'Mr Moon has left the stadium.' Payet loses possession and Deulofeu plays a great first-time ball through to Lukaku. The Everton striker has got behind Tomkins and Reid too easily and uses his pace and strength to round Adrián and tap home. That's his seventh goal in seven games against West Ham.

At half-time, we doubt if even Nigel's lucky banana can save us from the usual Everton comeback. We discuss Fraser's creative writing course; he has to rewrite the start of his Western novel as for some reason his tutors want to tweak his plot of ransoming a portly sheriff called Big Sam to an outpost in the north-east.

Payet only lasts five minutes of the second half and is replaced by Valencia. That looks ominous for Dimitri. At least Enner looks sharp and combines well with Lanzini, curling in a fine cross that Moses just fails to connect with. But his comeback only lasts ten minutes. Coleman makes a fair tackle, but Valencia falls awkwardly and has to be replaced by Zárate.

The ref continues to perplex. Lanzini shoots narrowly wide and West Ham's best chance comes after Moses wins a corner. Winston Reid's header is just over the bar. At the other end, Lukaku pokes a Galloway cross past the post.

At least we don't concede the usual late goal in the four minutes of added time, and if Payet hadn't been injured we might surely have won. The game ends in a draw and, in a nod to Bilić's heavy-metal football, the PA plays Black Sabbath's 'Paranoid' (a tribute to José Mourinho?) and Deep Purple's 'Highway Star', which pleases Nigel no end – this is a man who chose 'Smoke on the Water' for the romantic slow dance at his wedding.

I walk with Nigel to Plaistow and we agree that at least one point keeps the season ticking over and we are way ahead of relegation-certainties Chelsea. In fact, we go up to fifth, which causes a lot of celebration, as when I meet my family for a bonfire party in Warwick Avenue there are fireworks going off all over London.

However, on Monday comes the terrible news that Dimitri Payet might be out for three months with an ankle injury. That McCarthy foul could surely have been prevented if referee Paul Tierney had clamped down on some rough Everton tackling early in the game and issued a yellow card. Payet was running the midfield before being targeted by a reducer, for which McCarthy was only booked.

The only vaguely positive news is that at least we have two number ten-type players capable of playing Payet's role in Manuel Lanzini and Mauro Zárate, while Alex Song and Pedro Obiang will soon be available to boost the defensive midfield positions.

The key to West Ham's season will be how the side and manager react to this. It's time for the big squad to move into action and minimise the loss of a player who has been sensational so far. Last season, injuries gave the players an excuse to coast after Christmas – we can't let it happen this time.

To take my mind away from Payet's injury, there's a fine programme called *Goodbye to Boleyn* on Radio 4 later in the week, dealing with the impact that West Ham's move to Stratford will have on the environs of Green Street. It includes interviews with Nathan's pie and mash shop, burger sellers, programme sellers, Gary Firmager of *Over*

Land and Sea fanzine, Cynthia the hairdresser, who works in David Gold's old house at No. 442 Green Street, local residents, market traders and singing nuns Sister Immaculate and Sister Patricia, who live near the stadium. It's broadcast as part of Radio 4's *Lives in a Landscape* series and credit to producer Mark Burman for a great half-hour of radio. Radio 4, eh? We're now highbrow.

After the two weeks' international break it's off to the not-quite-so-lucky pub, the Hole in the Wall at Waterloo, for the live game at Spurs on Sunday. Fraser and Gavin (in flat caps), Matt, Lisa and Nigel are all present. There's a fine selection of real ales at the bar and the Gold Rush and Hogs Back TEA are both splendid compared to the Central's beers. Matt, Nigel and the Gav reminisce about Hatfield band Babe Ruth, as featured on BBC4's *Sounds of the '70s*. Nigel went to see Everton versus Aston Villa yesterday and Matt and Lisa have watched the WHU kids at Little Heath. The only problem is that we now have to watch a football match with West Ham Seniors. And we get thrashed 4-1, defending pretty terribly and looking lost without Payet. After an early-season slump, Harry Kane continues his revival with two goals.

The only plus at 4-0 down is Matt exclaiming, 'He's so

slow... I tell you, Jelavić will never score for us... What is Jelavić going to do with that?' as the substitute striker finds Lanzini with a fine through-ball and Manuel shoots into the top of the net. A consolation at least, as Matt is ribbed by all the TEA drinkers.

'Has any other club relied on any one player as much as we've relied on Dimitri Payet this season?' asks Nigel. Never mind Francis Crick and James Watson discovering DNA at the Eagle in Cambridge, we're asking the really big pub questions. Everything has been going through Dimitri and with numerous assists and five goals he's obviously going to be a massive loss. We decide that Man City rely on Agüero a lot, Spurs would miss Harry Kane and Everton Romelu Lukaku, but few teams have had such an obvious star. Just his presence seems to raise the game of the other players.

Still, the main problems were at the back against Spurs. We have some very good players to replace Payet. Manuel Lanzini is already having a fine season, Alex Song or Mauro Zárate can come into the midfield, Valencia will return in January, and there's the option of playing Carroll and Sakho together. Plus, there's £7 million Antonio and Jelavić desperate to get games.

But what we do need is a bit more creativity from Noble, Kouyaté and Moses to make up for his absence. And as *Match of the Day* points out, when teams press like Spurs did, the Hammers need to sometimes play the long ball out from the back to bypass the pressing gang. Even without Payet, we still have one of West Ham's strongest ever squads.

November ends with another disappointing home draw. Where's our famous Danny Dyer? There's a big queue of mainly female *EastEnders* fans outside the Newham Bookshop for Danny Dyer signing *Life Lessons from the East End* and I catch a glimpse of him through the open doors. Stef Dickers from the Bishopsgate Institute is helping to marshal the queue of Dyerites – a very upmarket bouncer. Vivian behind the counter says that Danny's been 'a real charmer'.

Then it's on to Ken's Café, which has been mentioned in an *Observer* feature by Daniel Taylor, including my comment that Carol is the best manager West Ham never had. Diego Costa wouldn't dare throw a bib at her as he did at the Chelsea bench last week. Taylor points out that a third of all clubs have now left their traditional stadiums and that a lot of memories will be lost and businesses closed down. Looking at West Ham's move, he covers all the right people around Upton Park, including Ken's Café, the Boleyn, the Black Lion, the Newham Bookshop, Nathan's Pies and Eels and Gary Firmager of *OLAS*. The informal tapestry of venues that has grown up around a ground is not easily replaced, and Taylor's piece makes many a reader feel a little misty-eyed.

Matt's arrived at 1 a.m. in his not-very-lucky Dukla Prague away shirt. He's been working nights and is about to fly to San Francisco for a fortnight. Meanwhile, Michael the Renaissance Man, Playwright and Whovian is arriving back from New York, but Matt says he's texted to say he's currently marooned at Heathrow. Nigel arrives late, telling us the tragic news that CQ has dropped and broken his favourite Enfield FC mug. I remind Matt about my bet that West Brom's Rickie Lambert will score more goals than Modibo Maïga. Thanks to the strange 2.05 p.m., TV-dictated kick-off time, Matt's food arrives late and he is forced to miss the kick-off.

Inside the stadium, none of the clocks are working. Added to the demolition of the 'Don't kill your wife, let us do it' sexist clock face outside the dry cleaners in Green Street, it's growing evidence of a time rift in E13 caused by West Ham's impending move and possible Zygon interference.

The Irons start off fairly well against a team with four giant centre-backs in defence, with Obiang looking solid in front of our back four, having replaced the suspended Noble. Rondón shoots just wide for WBA but that's their only threat. On seventeen minutes the ref does well to spot

McAuley holding Sakho just outside the penalty area and Zárate curls a lovely free kick into the top corner. It's the best goal of Zárate's Hammers career. Fraser, who should know better, declares: 'We've won it now, as in every game under Pulis this season only one team has scored.'

Kouyaté heads a good chance wide and Myhill saves with his legs as Lanzini shoots from distance after picking up a misplaced Albion pass. Zárate skilfully sets up Lanzini, whose shot produces another good save from Myhill.

'Can't Get Enough' by Bad Company comes on the PA at half-time, which impresses Nigel, and it all seems to be going well.

Albion bring on Rickie Lambert after the break and the big striker's arrival immediately brings results. The burly striker fires a hopeful shot that deflects off Winston Reid's arm and veers into the net. It's a fluke goal, but boosts Albion as West Ham's confidence falters.

Michael the Transatlantic Whovian arrives from Heathrow like an impending harbinger of dropped points, just after WBA equalise. Lambert has a free kick palmed wide by Adrián and the keeper then saves Rondón's free header with his chest.

Plan B is resumed, with Carroll coming on for Obiang. At least West Ham come back into it as Moses makes a great run from his own half and finds Sakho, who looks sure to score.

But McAuley makes a great challenge and Sakho goes down with what looks like a hamstring problem. He's replaced by Jelavić.

A week of night shifts, a late lunch, missing meeting the dad of Greenland's top indie band Nanook (unlike Nigel's wife CQ who's just visited Greenland) and watching West Ham trying to break down an eight-man defence proves too much for Matt, who memorably tirades at the ref, Jenkinson, Jelavić and myself for predicting that Lambert would turn his season around against West Ham. I try to tell Matt that there is actually a small possibility that what we say or do before the game doesn't affect the result. He's not having it.

Will a fortnight in the Hotel California with Lisa see him return with a more chillaxed attitude to West Ham's frailties and the negative karma of no Payet? Probably not if he still has to visit E13.

Near the end, Moses flashes a volley wide, but it ends up as a 1-1 draw. We walk to the Black Lion, where Gary O'Neil is on the box playing for Norwich and the Ridley's Old Bob is like nectar compared to the Central's offerings. We retreat to a windswept back bar covered in tarpaulins as the remains of Hurricane Barney batter the East End. Two of the walls have been demolished and it appears to be the remnants of the old boxing gym, with claret and blue paint still on the surviving walls. The Calais Jungle refugee camp vibe adds to the sense that all the facilities around Upton Park are slowly winding down.

Fraser muses: 'Will we win any games without Payet? Probably not.' A draw against a difficult Tony Pulis side isn't a disaster, but West Ham should surely have scored more in the first half. It's a trip to Old Trafford next. December could be a long month...

7

A CHRISTMAS CARROLL

WE'RE IN RYE, EAST SUSSEX, ENJOYING A ROMANTIC mini-break to celebrate our wedding anniversary as West Ham draw 0-0 at Old Trafford. It's a lovely old medieval town, once on the coast, but now inland on the flat atmospheric lowlands of East Sussex. Nicola and I are staying in Hayden's boutique B&B. There's real coffee on the dressing table and posh white dressing gowns in our wardrobe, while downstairs we are allowed unlimited coffee and chocolate cake.

Nicola's been taken to a gastro pub the night before while today we've explored the lovely old cobbles of Mermaid Street and visited the Mermaid Inn, once the haunt of vicious smugglers. We've climbed the narrow steps to the top of the tower of St Mary's Church, visited the museum in the historic Ypres Tower and explored lots of shops that sell candles, notepads and general fripperies. So I'm allowed to take a mini-break from romance and get the score at 4.30 p.m. from the TV in our room. On Radio London you can hear the West Ham fans chanting at the end of the match of 'Is this the Emirates?' and 'Is there a fire drill?'

After away wins at Arsenal, Liverpool and Man City, West Ham have been unlucky not to smuggle out three points from another giant club. Reid and Zárate both hit the post in the first half. Adrián's had to make some good saves late on, but the best chance fell to the Irons with Zárate skewing the ball horribly wide after a great lay-off from Andy Carroll. Still, a very credible point, particularly as Payet is missing and earlier that week Diafra Sakho has been ruled out for at least six weeks with a hamstring injury.

Matt's been having a romantic mini-break with Lisa too, and texts from the Hotel California: 'Local Man United fans are dancing in streets of Monterey CA at taking a point off West Ham.'

When we're back in London there's yet more bad news from the treatment room. Will the last fit player left at Chadwell Heath please turn out the floodlights? Manuel Lanzini is out for six weeks with a thigh injury sustained in training and Victor Moses, who pulled up in the first half at Old Trafford, could be out for a similar spell.

A couple of days later comes the news that now Winston Reid is out for six weeks as well, having suffered yet another muscle strain in training. All we need is a few teacup injuries and a bout of Devonshire Flu to round off the week. At least Bilić has identified the problem. He's brought forward West Ham's move to a new training ground at Rush Green to get away from Chadwell Heath. He tells the *Evening Standard* about the problems with the Chadwell Heath pitches: 'With Reid's injury, for example, they are slippery on the top but rock hard underneath, and it is a bad combination. We can live without the great dressing room, the kitchens and the free area for now.'

Though it does make you wonder why, in a multi-million-pound industry, we've been risking our prize performers on iffy training pitches.

West Ham now have Payet, Sakho, Lanzini, Moses and Reid out. The only good news is that Enner Valencia might be in contention for Saturday's match with Stoke.

We arrive for the Stoke game expecting a struggle. In Ken's Café, the *Whatever Happened to the Likely Lads* Christmas special is on the TV – that one where Bob has grown a beard – as another likely lad, Michael the Whovian, regales Nigel and his mate Michael the Plymouth Fan with the tale of how he's spotted the Lord High President of the Time Lords (aka actor Donald Sumpter) in the East Stand. If he really is a Time Lord perhaps Donald could extract Lionel Scaloni from his time stream a second before he boots the ball towards Steven Gerrard in the 2006 FA Cup Final...

Meanwhile, messages are coming through from Matt in California, who appears to have spent a little too long in Haight-Ashbury and now thinks that 'referees are beautiful people and every West Ham injury happens for a karmic reason'.

On the way to the ground, Michael manages to drop my Christmas card under a Stoke coach – the Stokies will probably assume 'wishing you no Christmas invasions' is a cryptic message from the ICF. Inside the East Stand, we meet Fraser, who is wearing his best Dexys Mac and planning to write the final 4,000 words of the first section of his novel after a cockney knees-up in the Central.

After Kouyaté has a shot parried, Stoke have a good half-hour with Afellay prospering against the unprotected Cresswell. Van Ginkel pokes a great chance wide and then Arnautović meets Afellay's cross and goes close under pressure from James 'Ginger Pelé' Collins. This gets a few 'Delilah's going in the away end.

Antonio makes one surging run on the right only to dither in the box, as slowly West Ham come back into it. Noble has a penalty claim denied while Aaron Cresswell's cross nearly reaches Antonio, who is thwarted by a desperate Stoke clearance.

Half-time sees Nigel get out his lucky banana and Matt text to say his whale-watching trip has been cancelled due to stormy weather, therefore, he quips, 'no chance of seeing Benni or Mido'.

West Ham really give it a go at the start of the second half. Ogbonna's long ball sees Antonio acrobatically volley, only for Butland to make another good stop. Butland shoves Carroll's header wide. Stoke's Arnautović has a free kick deflected against the bar, then Cresswell's cross-shot has to be palmed away by the excellent Butland.

It's turning into a really entertaining goalless draw as the festive crowd hollers 'Bubbles' and 'Come on you Irons!' Zárate makes some fantastic dribbles into the box, while Antonio is causing problems when switched to the left. Song appears close to returning to the form of last season, while Andy Carroll is looking fitter and more mobile, laying the ball off well and enjoying a good battle with Shawcross.

Hammers' old boy Glen Johnson crosses for Diouf to shoot, only for Adrián to make a great stop with his feet. With ten minutes to go in a finely balanced game, some strange people are leaving early, causing a row in front of us. This happens just as Zárate plays a one-two with Antonio and dribbles across the face of the area, firing a great effort against the foot of the post. That would have been a fantastic goal. From the second phase of that attack Tomkins crosses, Carroll wins the header and Valencia's poke towards goal is smothered by the City keeper again.

Antonio gets a big round of applause when subbed. He's the sort of trier the crowd will take to. His best performance since *Twelfth Night*. Stoke almost win it at the end as Arnautović finds Diouf but Adrián pulls off another great save. The excitement lasts to the end as in the fourth minute of added time Butland spills a cross, Tomkins heads back into the box and Kouyaté's header is cleared off the line. West Ham might not have won in six games (on the other hand we've drawn four of them), but it's been a game where both sides have given everything and West Ham are deservedly applauded off.

So it's the long walk to Plaistow Tube through darkened alleyways and back streets with Nigel and Michael the Plymouth Fan, and then on to dinner with WHU legend DC in Holloway. Fraser and Michael head to the Central, with Michael set to see Chas & Dave live, though the real attraction is the support, Darts. 'I'm happy that at least the points are still ticking over,' says Nigel. I'm inclined to agree.

The big news in the following week is the sacking of José Mourinho at Chelsea. That's the third manager West Ham have got sacked this season; Brendan Rodgers went soon after Liverpool lost 3-0 at home to the Irons and Dick Advocaat resigned as Sunderland boss after blowing a two-goal lead against the Hammers. Mourinho always looked in trouble after West Ham beat struggling Chelsea 2-1 back in October. Haranguing ref Jonathan Moss in his dressing room at half-time at Upton Park and reportedly calling him 'f**king weak' was particularly unnecessary. When Danny Dyer was then seen taking both the moral high ground and the proverbial out of José in the stand, you knew he had problems. Stamford Bridge is falling down, and I email various Chelsea fans with the suggestion that they might like to employ Avram Grant to finish off the job José started.

The last game before Christmas is a tame, goalless draw at Swansea. Catching the second half in my local before our Christmas drinks party, the main feature is that the excellent James Collins gets his head on everything and that Swansea's Gomis seems to have no understanding of the offside rule. Jelavić gets a full game as Carroll has strained his groin but looks rusty. It's so dull that for the second half Matt, Michael and Fraser, in a pub elsewhere, are reduced to trying to name 1970s bands that have re-formed with all their members still alive. Still, it's an away point, and this was a game for the depleted squad to make up with teamwork what they lacked in class.

Christmas arrives with a series of neighbourly drinks parties. Christmas dinner at our house in London and then a family trip to my brother and sister-in-law's gaff in Hertfordshire. On Boxing Day, the Hammers earn a 1-1 draw at Aston Villa after taking the lead through Aaron Cresswell, but conceding a soft penalty. It's West Ham's fifth successive draw, and an away point, but really we should be beating a bottom-of-the-table team that hasn't won in seventeen games, though then again it's the sort of game we used to lose.

That evening, though, something feels wrong. My throat feels like it's made of sandpaper, my head hurts and I can't finish the pint of Old Speckled Hen that Drew has just poured.

Despite an early night, I feel worse in the morning, alternating between chills and hot sweats. I've not felt this bad since relegation in 2011. Nicola is concerned that I'll infect her brother's young family and drives me to the station, where I return to London feeling terrible. I collapse into bed sucking a Fisherman's Friend (write your own joke here) and drinking Lemsip.

The next day it's an effort to get to the bathroom. This is

proper Flu and not Man Flu. I've got a deep, chesty cough that sends pains through my lungs. I'm not hungry and I'm off coffee and alcohol. But there's a game against Southampton today at 5.30 p.m. There's no way I should go; it could make me feel worse and I don't want to infect the East Stand. In any case a Google search on how flu is transmitted reassures me that if no one exchanges bodily fluids and I wash my hands a lot, my fellow season-ticket holders might be alright. This is stupid, but once you miss a game it's gone for ever. And I've paid fifty-odd quid for it. A couple of Lemsips might get me through it… So I take off my dressing gown, get dressed very slowly, put on extra scarves and walk slowly to the Tube feeling terrible.

Most football fans have that irrational fear that if they miss a game then their side will lose. West Ham need me if we are to get three points. I can still recall that dismal feeling of being away at university and sitting in the Battery pub in Morecambe as West Ham inexplicably lost 3-2 at home to Fulham in 1980 and blew promotion. It was down to me not being there.

I get to the game late so as to avoid infecting the diners in Ken's Café. Perhaps it's the flu, but walking down Green Street I find myself thinking that I don't want to leave. I can see all the arguments about transport and massive stadiums, but this is our home… It feels like walking to school with my daughters on the last day of primary school when they say they don't want to go to secondary school. Why can't everything remain the same?

After a quick bag search, it's through the turnstile and into the Upper East. Matt, Michael and Nigel arrive in their seats and tell me of strange happenings on the way to the East Stand.

'This is a good colour for your blog – there was a fan taking a dump behind one of the away coaches.' Apparently this was in the very same spot where Michael the Whovian had dropped my Christmas card on the day of the match against Stoke. Matt was so put off by the sight that he forgot to recycle his papers in the nearby council container. As the old chant goes: 'You're shit, aaaaargh!' Not the sort of new faeces we wanted to see at Upton Park in the transfer window.

Southampton should have an unassailable lead by half-time. The Saints go ahead after a lovely back-heel from Mané starts a move that sees Long cross low and Tadić bundle the ball in off Jenkinson.

Collins has to make a magnificent block to deny Davis. Ginger Pelé shows proper leadership by rollicking Zárate, Jenkinson and most of his teammates. It looks pretty scary as, with a quivering ginger beard, he berates Mauro. Ginge has signed a new contract this week, which is great news, as no doubt Big Sam would love to lure him to Sunderland. For all the technical ability of today's young stars, a lot of them seem to be lacking in character; Ginge has that in abundance and through sheer effort and leadership he inspires the men around him. On this form he has to stay in the team, even if it means dropping £10 million Ogbonna. And that Celtic-warrior beard must intimidate most strikers before a ball is kicked.

It's not going too well in this match, though: Jenkinson is out of position, having replaced the injured Cresswell at left-back; Song is off the pace; Noble is misplacing passes; and Zárate is having a frustrating game.

When the PA announces that Mr Moon has left the stadium, the Saints fans respond first with 'Mr Moon's a wanker!' and then, rather wittily, 'Mr Moon, he left 'cos you're shit!' But at least he didn't leave to defecate by one of the coaches.

Davis shoots just wide for Southampton and Adrián makes a couple of fine saves, including a tip-over from Fonte's header. Some boos can be heard as West Ham keep playing balls into touch.

It's so bad, Fraser quips at half-time, 'Can we have Allardyce back?' Bilić makes some sensible changes, switching Jenkinson to right-back and Tomkins to left-back, then bringing on the returning Carroll and Lanzini for Zárate and Song. We immediately look a better side and the crowd respond with some throaty roars. I've almost forgotten about my fever. Collins has a header cleared off the line and then Andy Carroll takes the ball off Tomkins's foot to blaze over when he should score.

It's hard to know how much longer is left as the scoreboards are still not working. Presumably Karren Brady didn't get enough Christmas Amazon vouchers to cover the cost of a replacement. Or maybe they just need a teenager to re-programme it if it's one of those new-fangled digital scoreboards.

But Hammers keep pressing, while Collins and Tomkins are solid at the back. Ginge plays on after injury and gets a rousing 'There's only one Ginger Pelé!' chant. Meanwhile, Matt remains strangely positive after his sojourn in California, even after Valencia is scythed down and the ref completely ignores it.

We equalise on sixty-nine minutes with a bizarre goal. The hardworking Michail Antonio runs into the box, takes a tumble and a defender's clearance bounces off his head into the net. It's Antonio's first for the club – and it's not even Twelfth Night yet. A comedy goal, but deserved on our second-half performance.

Ten minutes later it gets even better. Valencia crosses, the ball loops off a defender and Antonio heads onto the underside of the bar. Andy Carroll, sporting a new braided ponytail, does well to take a step back and head into the unguarded net. He runs to our section of the East Stand and does his runaway Virgin Pendolino slide towards the corner flag. Never in doubt!

'Oh when the Saints go 2-1 down!!' chant the gleeful Bobby Moore Stand.

Antonio then makes a thrilling run from the edge of his own area, outpacing the Saints' defence, before firing way wide. It shows his potential, though, and on a different night he might have had a hat-trick.

We hold on through four minutes of added time and at the whistle Bilić hugs every player. West Ham's first win in nine, though we're now unbeaten in six. And a much better return of four points from the two post-Christmas games, whereas last season we lost both of them. While we've had a proper floodlit atmosphere to prove what makes the Boleyn so special.

Football has acted as a tonic for my virus, though I start to feel rough on the Tube home, coughing and spluttering in the queue at Upton Park station. For the next week I'm in bed and even by the following Saturday I'm still feeling enervated despite some recovery. But there's another game to go to and I'm not missing Liverpool.

It's another TV-dictated kick-off time, this time 12.30 p.m., just to maximise the inconvenience for getting lunch or a pre-match beer.

Football really has changed. On the District Line there's a middle-aged couple in Barbours but wearing West Ham scarves, discussing buy-to-let deals. Then it's into Ken's Café, where Michael the Whovian is still waiting for his big breakfast before the imminent kick-off.

DC's been in, dispensing New Year's greetings with his two wee men. Nigel arrives late, still mourning the death of Motorhead's Lemmy and declaring that, even if he's too late for a cup of Carol's tea, 'That's the way I like it baby, I don't wanna live for ever!'

Sadly, Nigel's mum's hairdresser on the south coast hasn't come up with any tickets for the game at Bournemouth, despite Nigel offering to book us all in for a claret-and-blue rinse.

Inside Upton Park, there's an expectant atmosphere with Payet on the bench. Ibe shoots just past the post early on, but West Ham are then dominant. On ten minutes Antonio makes what looks like a great tackle to deny Moreno (it's actually a foul the replay on *MOTD* suggests) just outside WHU's box. From there West Ham counter swiftly, with Kouyaté finding Valencia on the right. Enner plays in a sumptuous cross for Antonio, who has rushed the length of the field, to stoop and head powerfully into the top of the net. A great goal.

Michael arrives just after Antonio's goal, having finally eaten his big breakfast in Ken's Café, but claims to have seen it on the TV in the concourse.

Lanzini jinks inside to send a swerving shot against the post, leaving Mignolet a bemused bystander. Andy Carroll is having a great game, winning the ball in the air against Lovren and Sakho and leading the line superbly. Noble, too, is all over the pitch. The only downside is when Lanzini has to go off with what appears to be more ligament trouble.

Liverpool do end the half with a lot of possession though, and after a nice passing move Can leans back to ping a shot onto West Ham's bar.

At half-time we discuss the *gegenpressing* issues of the day, such as Nigel's suggestion that Matt is carrying a man-bag (Nigel prefers a more prosaic plastic bag himself). Michael points out the Lord President of the Time Lords, aka the balding actor Donald Sumpter, in the bowels of the East Stand.

The Hammers start the second half well as rain sweeps the Boleyn and Jürgen Klopp gets wetter in his black anorak. When the ball falls to Noble on the right, he swings in a perfect cross. Andy Carroll rises like the Angel of North Essex, shoving Clyne and Valencia out of the way and powering in an unstoppable header as Mignolet appears to be trying to hail a bus back to Merseyside. AC runs to the East Stand and slides belly-first towards the corner flag, again leaving two great ruts in the pitch. Lovely moment for Big Andy. The Bobby Moore Stand enjoys a rousing chorus of 'Andy Carroll – he left 'cos you're shit!' aimed at the Scousers.

It gets better when Payet comes on for Valencia after sixty-four minutes to a rousing 'We've got Payet!' from all four corners of the ground. Dimitri's in tears at the reception. Purist Matt becomes rather agitated that the song speeds up at the end, in violation of the original Billy Ray Cyrus tune. I explain that, rather like Elvis Costello, the West Ham fans like to constantly rework old songs and challenge themselves musically.

Dimitri's first touch is to feint past three Liverpool players and bring gasps of delight from the crowd. It feels like a special season again now Dimitri's back. Bilić did well to have the side still taking points during that Payet-less, winless spell of eight games. Payet then sets up Cresswell for a cross and Andy Carroll's header is pawed away by Mignolet; Antonio shoots from the rebound but the keeper blocks it again. Close.

We cede a lot of possession to Liverpool and they improve a bit when Smith and Lallana come on. Noble has to head off the line and Allen heads a good chance wide. But at the other end Payet plays a fine through-ball to the onrushing Kouyaté, who fires at a good height for Mignolet to save.

Sub Jenkinson fouls his man when he should hold it up

in the corner, prompting a brief tirade from Matt, until he remembers that he's being positive and mutters, 'Unlucky, Jenks!'

By added time we're confident enough to sing 'Can we play you every week?'

It's West Ham's first league double over Liverpool since 1963 and it's accompanied by the Beatles, with 'Twist and Shout' playing on the PA.

Recovering from flu, I shun the pub as the Central's beers might finish me off, but do drop into the Newham Bookshop to pick up a copy of the excellent book *Upton Park Memories*, which includes a few of my own. And we've just seen another of those memories today. I'm not sure what there is to moan about now. We go sixth. And it's after Christmas.

It's been a really impressive performance from Andy Carroll. It wasn't just his goal; he looked more mobile than he has for a long time, terrorising the Liverpool defence and also doing some great defensive work at corners.

Though, as several papers report, there was a post-match warning from Slaven Bilić to keep working hard: 'He looks really good and fit and it's all about him now. Is he going to maintain and progress and look after himself, or is he going to go the other way? He has history in that and I'm not his dad, I can't demand things from him. But I'm expecting that to be fair.'

Monday's *Guardian* also notes that Sam Allardyce said in his autobiography of Carroll: 'He treats life too casually. He also gets himself into situations off the pitch which a manager can do without – and so can he.'

There's a hint of Frank McAvennie about Carroll. I like the fact that he plays football with a smile like the working-class players of old and dates *TOWIE* babes. We can't all be James Milner. But clearly, at twenty-six, such an injury-prone player has to work really hard from now on. If he continues to play like he did against Liverpool, he can be unstoppable and he might finally develop into the complete striker that we've been looking for. Or he might get injured again...

8

MY DAD'S LAST GAME

THE FESTIVE FIXTURES REMIND ME OF THE LAST TIME I took my dad to Upton Park. It was a Boxing Day fixture against Portsmouth in 2006. The first game he took me to was a home match against Blackpool in 1970, thirty-six years earlier. Back then we were still promiscuous football fans, searching for a club, touring the teams of London. But soon we settled on West Ham as our London side.

Once, my dad had taken me to football matches, and now I was taking him. He was seventy-nine and hadn't been to West Ham for twenty years. And I had to do all the things my dad used to do for me, like making sure he didn't get lost in the crowd, that he didn't lose anything or have to stand for too long on the Tube or get pushed over in the rush to leave the stadium.

My mum had died last September. The certainties of my dad's life had gone. They were together for fifty-three years and he relied on her for everything – cooking, washing, housekeeping and emotional support. He'd been trying to forget that she wasn't at home by going to pub lunches, attending Masonic meetings and visiting the Lewes fireworks. He'd even told me that, after his difficult early childhood, my mum was his 'saviour'.

My dad had been staying with us in London over Christmas and had encountered numerous things alien to his life in rural Norfolk – a gay vicar in a church with incense, assertive women and, more positively for him, exotic new food such as Kettle Chips and hummus and an Algerian barber in Blackstock Road who gave him a £3 haircut.

'What time are we going to the match tomorrow?' he asks at Christmas lunch. For the rest of the meal he sits staring into space and then tears trickle down his cheek. He proposes a toast to 'she who is immortal'. My daughters hug him and in turn start crying for Granny Sheila. It's hard to see the man whose values I spent much of my youth challenging now seeming so vulnerable.

Football was the bond my father and I had always shared, albeit in a taciturn, male kind of way. My dad was a tenant farmer in Essex, close enough to London to see the Post Office tower on a clear day. The farm was later dissected by the M25, but he always insisted that I had to be a farmer. I knew I wanted to be a writer. For the past twenty years, since he gave up his farm, he'd managed to get 'Well, if Pete had gone in for farming…' into nearly every conversation. My mum was always the mediator.

My dad came from a generation of men who didn't play with children. But when, at the age of eleven, I took an interest in football, he decided to take me to some matches. He'd never shown any interest in football before, but we visited various London grounds, then became regulars at West Ham. When I became a teenager and wanted to go with my mates, he went on his own, getting to know some of the fans who stood near him on the North Bank.

Then came university and a career in journalism. In the 1980s I was an anti-Thatcher, post-punk, CND-supporting leftie, while my dad was a Thatcher-loving, *Telegraph*-reading Conservative. His main interest was Freemasonry and then, after holidays in Northern Ireland, he became a fan of Ian Paisley, joined an Orange lodge and played the flute in an Orange band based in Corby. Discussing West Ham's relegation prospects was our one neutral topic of conversation.

My mum, born in Stoke, had always taken an interest in the results and became a proxy Hammers fan. In September, we had spent a horrible week by her hospital bedside. She had Alzheimer's disease, needed a hip operation and had just been operated on for a burst stomach ulcer. But, after two days in critical care, she came round. She was hopelessly confused and kept worrying about where the family were going to eat, asking, 'Shall we go to the Anvil [the local pub]?' Then she suddenly said, 'I support West Ham!' It was a sign that she knew I was there. Two days later, her body gave up and she died.

So now we're leaving for the match once more. Perhaps there were other generations of my dad's family who visited West Ham. His father, Sidney, died before I was born, but once he had moved to middle-class Upminster he didn't, as far as I know, show any interest in football. But he grew up close to the ground in Forest Gate and East Ham and had business premises close to the ground. Surely he must have been to the odd game or two before enlisting for the First World War. While my great-grandfather Alfred was raised on Commercial Road (his father was a saddler who died from tuberculosis at the age of thirty-three) and might well have seen the formative years of Thames Ironworks and West Ham.

My dad negotiates the stairs at the Tube slowly but steadily as I hold his arm. Thankfully, a train arrives within two minutes. Because of his arthritis, my dad, who completed the London marathon at the age of fifty-eight, now walks with a stick. A young Chelsea fan, on his way to Stamford Bridge, spots this and offers him his seat. Increasingly, my dad has found security in maps. Now he wants to know the name of every station we pass through. 'Is this the Holborn Line?' he asks. 'No,' I respond, 'this is the Victoria Line.'

Standing above him, I repeat the name of every station until Oxford Circus. We negotiate shopping crowds, stairs and a long corridor on our way to the Central Line. The next change at Mile End is simply a matter of crossing platforms – my worries about crowds, stairs and transfers are now exactly the same as when my daughters were in the buggy stage.

At Mile End, my father says he could do with a loo, because the tablets he's taking to counter the beta-blockers he's on make him want to go to the toilet more often than normal. But he thinks he can hold out until Upton Park. We leave Upton Park station, finding only an out-of-order public loo in Green Street market, so instead sneak into the gents in the Queen's pub.

That emergency over, we head for Ken's Café. We sit at a table and drink steaming mugs of strong tea. 'You'd see the ball come out of the tunnel first, then Bobby Moore, and the goalkeeper, Bobby Ferguson, was always behind him,' recalls my dad, thinking of our first visits here in 1970.

'We'll wait a long time for Bobby Moore to come out today,' he mutters and his eyes are moist again. Maybe he's thinking of my mum and how alone he feels, the great Bobby Moore's premature death from bowel cancer, the passing of time, the boy who's grown into a middle-aged man. I wonder how many other fans were having intimations of mortality in Ken's Café.

We arrive in the ground early to beat the crowds. It's half an hour until kick-off, but the players are already warming up. I show my dad the old North Bank, now the Centenary Stand, where he used to watch behind the goal. Sometimes we even spotted him on TV as we watched the *Big Match* after Sunday dinner. Once he had his cash half-inched from his back trouser pocket, a traumatic experience for a cattle dealer, and ever since he'd used a safety pin to secure his wallet inside his jacket.

My dad went to Brentwood School and I introduce him to my fellow season-ticket holder Nigel, who is also an old Brentwood. He's pleased I'm mixing with the right sort. There's an emotional chorus of 'I'm Forever Blowing Bubbles' from 34,913 fans and then the game kicks off. West Ham are lethargic and let in a soft goal from Linvoy Primus. And then Portsmouth score an almost identical goal through another Primus header from a free kick. Dodgy goals, relegation struggles – it's almost as if my dad has never left. The man behind is hollering expletives. At forty-seven, I still don't swear in front of my dad, but I'm reminded of the childhood frisson of standing on the North Bank with him and hearing adults hollering f-words.

At the start of the second half, my dad joins in with the crowd's a-cappella chorus of 'Bubbles'. Alan Curbishley has brought on Carlos Tevez for Matthew Etherington. Tevez makes a difference; he's obviously a world-class player and no one can understand why he's not in the side. West Ham pull a goal back late on through Teddy Sheringham.

My dad's involved in the game, in the present, which is good; in recent months much of his time had been spent worrying about future events: whether his alarm will go off, how he'll get two suitcases on the train and whether his cleaner is coming on Wednesday.

West Ham lose, but for forty-five minutes nothing else has mattered. When the final whistle blows, I help my dad down the steep exit steps. He finds it difficult, bending down, his hands trembling with the effort. He used to rush from games to catch the fast train from Barking to Upminster. Maybe one day it will be my daughters helping their old man after the inevitable West Ham defeat, holding up the impatient fans behind.

I'm thinking of other exits from matches. My mum would be waiting at home in the farmhouse with steak and chips and a note of the other football results. Sometimes we'd even make it back in time for the end of *Doctor Who*. Later we attended floodlit games, driving home from the Tube, headlights on silver birches, the shutting of the farm gate, logs still burning in the fireplace, the breakfast table set. As Madness once put it, 'She's the one they're going to miss in lots of ways.'

Back in north London, we stop at my local for a pint, as we used to once by Upminster station. Maybe I should tell him that I understand it was disappointing for him that I never became a farmer; maybe he should tell me that he thinks I can write. Maybe we should discuss how much we miss my mum. But for now our closeness comes from the league table on the screen flickering in the corner.

'I can't see them staying up on that form,' says my dad. 'They're averaging less than a point a game.'

My dad died in September the following year. My sister and I had left him that lunchtime and returned to London. That evening he'd poured himself a pint of beer. Hopefully he had a sip or two before suffering a stroke. He was found by his cleaner the next day. We rushed to hospital but he died a day later.

I've still got my dad's old West Ham programmes in the attic, complete with his team changes written in Biro. He kept them by his bed and I find myself doing likewise with mine.

We spent a lot of time discussing West Ham's underachievement and why Bobby Ferguson could take such massive goal kicks. My dad would never have thought that the Boleyn itself would one day disappear.

Though, as a studier of Tube maps, my dad might well have approved of the better transport links of the new Olympic Stadium and, as a cattle dealer, he'd certainly have liked getting a used stadium on the cheap.

Still, a lot of family history must be floating around the ether of the Boleyn Ground. Countless families must have found closeness through football. And when it's all a housing estate, perhaps a part of my dad will still be lingering on the spot that used to be the North Bank.

9

JE T'AIME, DIMITRI

AFTER A SUPERB START TO THE NEW YEAR BEATING Liverpool, it's the slightly diminished magic of the FA Cup and a home tie against Championship side Wolves the following Saturday.

The previous day's *Daily Telegraph* has included an interview with Super Slaven Bilić, in which he compared managing West Ham to buying a dog. When asked about the risks of possibly tarnishing the fans' memories of his West Ham playing career, Bilić replies: 'When you are buying a dog you find like this – ten reasons not to buy it. Because you can't go out more, if you are travelling it's a problem, he's going to pee there and there until he learns. He's going to bite your cat, he's going to leave your place smelly. But there is one reason that's good – he loves you, he loves you. He gives you love. Every time you come home it's like it's the first time he's seen you... So like this with West Ham. There was, there still is, and it's always going to be [a risk].'

An interesting canine analogy, particularly when you remember West Ham had Martin 'Mad Dog' Allen in the early 1990s. Slaven would probably have given Martin a good pat and a new blanket to worry.

Slaven also speaks a lot of sense about not complicating the game with philosophies and methodologies: 'So I can use those scientific words every day and people will probably think "oh, yeah". But I prefer to talk simply. Because for me football is a very simple sport. But people are trying to ... make it like "big-time complicated".'

⚽ ⚽ ⚽

My first stop of the day for the Wolves match is at the Newham Bookshop, where Brian Williams, author of *Nearly Reach The Sky*, is with his wife Di signing books amid manager Vivian Archer's Dickensian towers of literary tomes. Brian even buys a copy of my own *Flying So High: West Ham's Cup Finals*. 'Between us we might soon have the complete lyrics to "Bubbles" in book titles,' he suggests.

It's amazing how many books Vivian manages to cram

into her tiny shop and yet still know where everything is. Every surface is covered with paperbacks. On leaving, my bag catches one of the many piles of books by the till. A literary avalanche ensues, causing momentary chaos as I'm buried in West Ham-themed books, literary fiction, quiz books and stocking fillers. Thankfully Vivian soon restores order to her shelves as I shamefacedly pick up paperbacks and restore a Bobby Moore biography to its shelf.

Then it's on to Ken's Café, where we're joined by Nigel's mate Adrian, a devoted Wolves fan (and dedicated reader of my blog Hammers in the Heart). Adrian has the bemused air of a typical football fan and every summer threatens to give up his Wolves season ticket. He never does and still travels from his base in Exeter to Molineux for every home match, claiming it's mainly to see his mum. He's not optimistic about today's match as Wolves have just sold their best striker, Afobe, to Bournemouth and have 'a bloke up front who's hardly played for two years'.

Michael the Whovian has actually got his big breakfast in early, but Matt, Lisa and Nigel are left waiting until 2.45 p.m., so it's a late dash down Tudor Road for the East Stand.

The first half is pretty tedious, though astonishingly enough the scoreboard is working again.

Wolves have come to frustrate. West Ham have too many holding midfielders and Jelavić is starved of service and doesn't look sharp. Obiang has a shot saved and late on Jenkinson – whose crossing has been poor – has a fine shot tipped over by Ikeme, and that's about it.

At half-time the PA plays Led Zeppelin's 'Whole Lotta Love' with lead vocals by Robert Plant, a well-known Wolves fan, says Nigel.

Early in the second half, the PA announces that 'Mr Moon is in the stadium' and then 'Mr Moon has left the stadium'. The Wolves fans amuse themselves by singing, 'Who the f**k is Mr Moon?' and then 'Mr Moon is a wanker, is a wanker!' – which is a bit offensive towards our much-loved security expert.

'Just imagine, this could be the last time we watch West Ham struggle to beat a lower division side at the Boleyn,' I muse ruefully.

James Collins makes a fine last-ditch clearance to deny Wolves. Another great moment from Ginge. Earlier in the week, Garth Crooks had said Collins reminded him of Gandalf. Indeed, with his mighty ginger beard, James could easily be a character from *The Lord of the Rings* repelling rampaging Orcs. Perhaps he should apply for special dispensation to play with a staff in his hand.

Payet comes on and so does Andy Carroll, which immediately improves the Irons. Payet hits a free kick onto the roof of the net and Pedro Obiang has a shot just wide.

Just as I'm saying that Jelavić is down to four out of ten

and they'll be dancing in the streets of Exeter, the curse of Mystic May strikes in the eighty-fifth minute. Carroll finds Jelavić on the edge of the area and the Croatian strikes a sublime half volley into the corner of the net before celebrating in our corner of the East Stand. A class finish and more like the Jelavić we remember from Everton days.

'We never doubted you, Captain Jelavić,' suggests Private Michael, who had earlier thought we were all doomed. To think that Matt had suggested Jelavić would never score for the Hammers…

'How shit must you be, it's only 1-0?' chant the away fans.

There's time for le Fondre to put a good chance wide at the end and then that's it, we're through to the next round.

'I wonder if Millwall are still in the draw,' opines Fraser.

We head to the Central where for once they've got enough staff on. 'After all these years they've discovered why all these strangers keep turning up on a Saturday afternoon,' I suggest.

Over our pints, Michael confesses that he's resisted the January sale in the club souvenir shop – even the WHU dog bowls. Adrian arrives from the away end and accepts defeat stoically before he and Nigel head off to relive the game in a Swedish-themed restaurant in Kew (perhaps they play Abba?).

So, just another four games to go before it's the inevitable Cup Final breakfast at Nigel's gaff. We had a successful

Play-Off Final breakfast at Nigel's in 2005, and ever since we've been predicting a pre-final trip to Kew for poached eggs on toast. One year it might actually happen.

After the Wolves game there's more bad news on Manuel Lanzini. Having been injured against Liverpool, he's now out for another six weeks. Was he rushed back too soon? Still, at least Andy Carroll hasn't been crocked again. Yet…

Twelve minutes into the midweek match at Bournemouth, Big Andy runs down the wing to get in a dangerous cross, but immediately pulls up with a hamstring injury and could be out for four to six weeks.

I'm listening to the game on Radio London. The Cherries take the lead as Harry Arter twists and turns on the edge of the area to score with a shot that perhaps Adrián should have saved. The home side should go two up when Afobe heads over from two yards out. The Hammers do have a few chances in the first half, with Boruc making a great save from Jelavić's deflected cross and then tipping over from Payet.

The old West Ham would have slumped to a defeat against the plucky new boys, but not this side. Second half it all comes up claret thanks to the genius of Payet. Antonio is fouled on the edge of the box and the Reunion man fires an incredible Beckham-esque free kick up and over the wall and in off the underside of the bar, before being booked for jumping in with the celebrating West Ham fans. Goal of the season so far and it's brilliant to hear the resounding choruses of 'We've got Payet!' on the radio.

The French magician then manages to twist past three defenders on the right, including what appears to be a back-heeled rabona (something which sounds more like a 1980s cocktail) and presents Enner Valencia with a tap-in. Payet, still not completely match-fit, is then subbed and goes off to a big hug from Slaven in his beanie hat.

Antonio wins another free kick and Enner Valencia fires a dipping effort over the wall and into the net, leaving the bemused Artur Boruc looking like a man whose bus has just completely ignored his request to stop. Enner's never done that before. Payet is making everyone else in the side play better too.

West Ham are now unbeaten in nine games and it's a great three points on the south coast. We're fifth and our season is back on course. And it's been a bad night for Nigel's mum's hairdresser, who, rather than getting us tickets, was taking his new girlfriend to the match on a hot date … only to see his boys receive a right haircut.

So it's probably all going too well and seasoned fans kind of expect a defeat at struggling Newcastle. I receive the news on my iPhone while at the Sir Stanley Spencer art gallery at Cookham. We're on one of Nicola's improving winter walks by the Thames in scenic Berkshire.

The Irons are unfortunate to come across Newcastle's new £12 million signing, Jonjo Shelvey – a Harold Wood boy as well as a Lord Voldemort doppelgänger – who has points to prove to old club Swansea and new boss Steve McClaren. Shelvey dominates the first half and West Ham are two down at the break. Jelavić comes on for the second half and scores with his first touch, when he gathers Mbemba's poor back pass, rounds the keeper and slots home. The Hammers play better in the second half, though Newcastle have chances to get a third as Adrián makes two good stops from Mitrović and Wijnaldum slews wide. Late on Jelavić gets in a great centre and Kouyaté's header is saved by Elliot's knee.

But it ends 2-1 and Steve McClaren, the Wally with the Brolly, has finally beaten Super Slav, watched by the unlikely duo of Alan Shearer and Ed Sheeran, who just might be the Geordies' best double act since Ant and Dec. Had we avoided defeat it would have been a club record – nine matches undefeated in the Premier League. Hard to complain too much after our recent run, but now it's time to regroup.

We also see some transfer activity in the January window. Mauro Zárate is, a little surprisingly, sold to Fiorentina for a fee of around £1.5 million. Should we have let Zárate go or kept him for the rest of the season, particularly with Sakho and Carroll out? Mauro had problems with Big Sam, Harry Redknapp and Chris Ramsey last season, but under Slaven has looked a player again. He's scored quality goals against Arsenal, Chelsea and West Brom, got the equaliser at Leicester in the League Cup and netted a fine solo effort against FC Astra in the Europa League. And at times, as against Stoke, he's looked a real quality player, though in other matches he could be infuriatingly selfish and drift out of games.

Part of the Zárate money goes towards buying right-back Sam Byram from Leeds for £3.7 million. My Leeds-supporting pal Anthony Clavane, author of *The Promised Land*, is distraught that Byram is leaving and apparently there have been comparisons with Gareth Bale made due to his surging runs down the right. Byram will compete with James Tomkins and Carl Jenkinson for the right-back spot.

It's good to discover Byram is an Essex man, born in Thurrock, though his family later moved to Yorkshire. He should have a feeling for the club as there are quite a few Irons in his family. Sam tells the *Evening Standard*: 'My uncle and my cousin are big West Ham fans and have bought their tickets for the new stadium. My uncle was down here yesterday getting a shirt with my name on the back.'

Meanwhile, Zárate is replaced by the loan signing of Fenerbahçe striker Emmanuel Emenike. Emenike previews his move by tweeting a still from the film *Green Street* – though perhaps someone should tell him that neither Elijah Wood nor Frodo Baggins are West Ham fans in real life.

The injured Diafra Sakho has hit the wall though. A full-page in the *Evening Standard* reports that Sakho has crashed his Lamborghini through a garden wall in Hornchurch after colliding with another car and spinning off the road. Thankfully no one was hurt, though Diafra's motor is a write-off. And it turns out the garden wall he crashed into was at the home of a West Ham fan, who immediately recognised him.

For the Manchester City home game, I've acquired a pair of tickets for the Betway Stand, and I'm taking my seventeen-year-old daughter Lola to what could be her final match at Upton Park. Politics is her latest love and I wonder if Dimitri Payet can compete with Jeremy Corbyn. It seems hardly any time since I was taking her to her first game against Man City, aged four, having 'sloppy egg' in Ken's Café and enjoying a 4-0 win against Wigan in the Championship. When she enthused about Marlon Harewood and I began to forget that we'd sold Ferdinand, Lampard, Cole and most of the England team.

In Ken's Café, Matt has forgotten his unlucky Dukla Prague away shirt, while Nigel and his wife CQ have forgotten CQ's not-very-lucky aniseed balls. Michael the Whovian has got his big breakfast in early, but tells us that he's unsure about Chris Chibnall, Steven Moffat's newly announced successor as *Doctor Who* showrunner.

We discuss the recent death of David Bowie and wonder if David supported his local Crystal Palace side, or maybe Chelsea.

'He didn't like football at all – hardly any rock stars did in the 1970s,' says Matt.

'He went to a game once, but was put off by too many programme ch-ch-changes,' I quip.

Lola becomes quite tearful thinking this might be the last time she visits Upton Park and has egg, chips and beans with two slices of toast and a cup of tea in Ken's. Then CQ quizzes her on Momentum (the group of youngish Corbyn supporters within the Labour Party) in the political salon that is Ken's – the 21st-century equivalent of tea at Samuel Johnson's house.

On the way to our new seats, we bump into my old school mate Steve, up from Cornwall for the match – though I'm not sure if he's in a box with Russell Brand and Noel Gallagher, he could just be with Alison and Scott.

We have a great view of the players and mascots coming

out of the tunnel and, going through the pre-match presentations, Lola notes from a feminist perspective that she's surrounded by middle-aged white men.

It's the usual slow start. From the kick-off Kouyaté leaves Touré looking less mobile than the Belly Busters burger stall on Green Street, as the West Ham man speeds past him on the left and crosses into the box. Valencia is lurking on the edge of the area and prods home under Hart. This is after a mere fifty-three seconds. 'It's not always like this!' I tell my disbelieving daughter. Upton Park bounces to our new theme song of 'We've got Payet! Dimitri Payet! I just don't think you understand…' I can't remember when I heard the Boleyn Ground so positive – perhaps in 2006 in the weeks before the FA Cup Final.

Or perhaps we've just antagonised City. They play some crisp, fluid stuff going forward and Agüero produces a brilliant lob that bounces off Adrián's post, before Reid chests it back to the grateful custodian. After seven minutes, Agüero breaks on the left and Jenkinson takes player and ball for a softish-looking penalty. Agüero duly dispatches and the City fans sing, 'We're not really here!' It's been some start to the match.

Instead of crumbling, though, the Hammers come right back. Payet looks better than Kevin De Bruyne, Yaya Touré, David Silva and all the rest of City's superstars.

In our borrowed West Stand seats we have a great view of the managers. City's Pellegrini stands on the touchline with the air of a kindly uncle watching the young folk dancing at a wedding, while Slaven Bilić is much more animated. He stands right on the line, pumping his fists, waving his arms and sitting on his haunches. In his black suit and tie he looks rather like a City trader who's just seen all his Chinese shares short sold and is complaining about it to the fourth official.

Jenkinson only lasts another couple of minutes before departing with what looks like a bad injury. On comes young Sam Byram to replace him. 'Dad, he looks about twelve!' protests Lola. Sam's first touch is to instantly control a strange high ball from Payet and play it sixty yards back to the Reunion man. Byram looks instantly at home against City and we might have a player. He's not afraid to clatter the odd winger either and picks up a yellow card later on.

Kouyaté gets fouled and requires treatment, which the ref completely ignores, earning a chorus of 'You're not fit to referee!' After half an hour Payet plays Antonio through with a brilliant shimmy and pass. Demichelis is lucky only to be booked as he brings down the flying Shakespearian winger on the edge of the box. Antonio would surely have got a shot in. From the resulting free kick, Hart produces a brilliant one-handed save to stop Payet's effort going in the top corner.

We go in level at half-time and we have a good view of ex-Hammer Jack Collison being interviewed on the pitch. Matt texts from the East Stand to say that he's losing his LA vibes and 'the ref is having a shocker!'

Delph shoots against the outside of the post for City after the restart, just after Mr Moon has left the stadium. Strange he should scarper, as it's a cracking game. The busy Antonio heads wide of the left post after a West Ham corner. Ten minutes into the second half Antonio takes a long throw, Otamendi is caught looking for planetary alignments in the night sky and Valencia nips behind him to prod past Hart and runs to a joyous bank of Bobby Moore Stand fans. That's four in three games for Enner now.

It looks like it could be another amazing victory. Noble has an immense game and is all over the pitch. Song is inspired, breaking up numerous attacks on the edge of WHU's box, while Kouyaté is having a fine game too.

But City bring on £50 million Raheem Sterling and youngster Kelechi Iheanacho and always look dangerous. When Victor Moses comes on for Antonio we briefly have Moses and Jesus on the same pitch, surely enough to please Matt the Vicar's Son in the East Stand. City equalise when Iheanacho makes a run into West Ham's box, the ball inadvertently rebounds off Cresswell and Agüero shows his class to balance himself and chip over Adrián.

It's end to end for the final ten minutes, but we can be proud of the way West Ham have matched the Champions of two seasons ago. In added time Agüero puts a chance straight at Adrián. With seconds to go, substitute Victor Moses is brought down by Fernando as West Ham attack towards the Bobby Moore Stand. From Payet's free kick Kouyaté heads against the top of the bar. A big 'Oooohhhh!' resonates around the Boleyn. It's the last action of the match.

What a game. It feels like one of those classic draws from 1970s, where the crowd has gone home thoroughly entertained and the fact that we haven't won doesn't matter too much. I take a picture of Lola in her West Ham scarf and her mum's brown Arthur Daley cashmere coat as we leave. There's a hubbub of drained excitement as we trek through the never-ending alleyways beyond Walton Road and head to Plaistow Tube. It's a good day to be a Hammers fan and another sign we've got a team here.

On that night's *Match of the Day* it's a little worrying that the pundits are starting to wake up to the skills of Dimitri Payet. The *Evening Standard*'s Patrick Barclay has suggested he should be in the running for the Footballer of the Year trophy. We don't want to alert the world's elite clubs to just how good he is. The Champions League clubs must also be looking at Dimitri enviously. He would certainly improve Man United or Liverpool and would fit into the Arsenal and

Man City teams easily enough, as well as most of Europe's elite sides.

Thankfully, Slaven Bilić has said that 'no money in the world' would tempt West Ham to sell Payet and Sullivan and Gold seem to realise that we have to hold on to him. We have the lure of the Olympic Stadium to keep Payet at the club and the possibility of European football. And he seems genuinely moved by the love of the fans, saying he's never had his own song before; there surely isn't another club that would give him his own song to the tune of 'Achy Breaky Heart'.

The bad news for Bilić is that Carl Jenkinson is out for the season following his injury against City. It's his cruciate ligament and Jenks has returned to Arsenal. A real shame, as although he's not been as impressive as last season, he's always given it everything and has scored twice this season. Just as well West Ham have signed Sam Byram and have James Tomkins ready to fit in at right-back.

January ends with a tricky-looking away tie at Liverpool in the FA Cup. So it's off to the lucky/unlucky pub the Hole in the Wall at Waterloo, where our posse has seen West Ham both win at Arsenal and get thrashed at Spurs. Fraser and myself opt for the Jurassic ale, which has kept pretty well over the millennia. Matt and Lisa are at the game, having opted for a romantic mini-break in a boutique hotel. Matt texts to tell me they're 'on the 26 bus to Anfield, soft lad'.

Liverpool play a very weakened side full of kids and squad players as they have a League Cup semi-final coming up. Even so, West Ham are indebted to a fine performance from reserve keeper Darren Randolph. It's not a great game and for much of it Fraser, in the second year of his Creative Writing MA, is left rehearsing his cowboy accent for the reading of his Western to a bunch of 'goddam literary agents', while Michael is high on steroids for his sinus condition, which is probably just as well. Randolph makes a good stop from Teixeira and a great triple save, denying Benteke and then blocking two follow-ups.

It ends 0-0, which is a good result, though also feels like a missed opportunity as only Mignolet and Clyne were Liverpool regulars. Perhaps it's a sign of progress to be upset at not beating Liverpool for a third time in one season. So now it's back to Upton Park for the replay.

February begins with a Tuesday night game against bottom-of-the-table Aston Villa at Upton Park. These games are never easy though.

Inside Ken's Café, Lisa is ordering cheesy chips and Billy is shouting, 'I can't get through, I'm trapped!' as he tries to return with his plates past a burgeoning queue. Michael the

Renaissance Man arrives late and, in a triumph of optimism over experience, orders a big breakfast thinking he'll make the kick-off. His Irons constitution manages to cope with some remarkably rapid ingestion before we leg it down the alleyway. As the café empties, Carol offers to give Michael special treatment next time: 'Just for once we'll make sure he sees the kick-off!' There's a rare appearance of Kenneth himself from the back of the kitchen to greet his best customers.

Within the East Stand, the big news is that Fraser has opted for the *Steptoe and Son* look with a rakish neck scarf. West Ham start very slowly and the whole side looks jaded – possibly not surprising after a testing game at Anfield and with Tomkins playing with thirteen stitches in a head wound from the Liverpool game and Kouyaté still feeling Saturday's injury – with Villa shading it in the first ten minutes. An optimistic penalty appeal against Antonio is turned down after the ball hits his hand. But Villa's game plan is ruined when Jordan Ayew stupidly elbows Cresswell in the face after seventeen minutes. The crowd in the corner of the Bobby Moore Stand certainly spot it and the ref gives Ayew a straight red. He wasn't provoked and it's absolute stupidity. It's noticeable he didn't try to do it to Collins or Tomkins.

Nothing much else happens in the first half. Tomkins's shot is headed over by Valencia and Enner hits a forty-yard free kick just wide and that's it. Even Payet is anonymous.

Playing against ten men who are bottom of the league. What could possibly go wrong? Surely it won't be like the Hull game two seasons ago.

Part-time Nigel turns up in the bowels of the East Stand at half-time complaining about the Tube and saying he's almost glad we're going to the superior transport hub of Stratford. The absent Matt is preparing for his night shift by watching the game in the pub and seems to have lost all his positivity, texting, 'Have our players bet on who can play worst? Think Antonio is winning, but it's very close.'

But the Hammers start much more positively in the second half, penning Villa back. Mark Noble produces a tremendous volley straight from a corner, only to see it brilliantly saved by Bunn. Payet hits the post with a free kick and Richards makes a great clearance from Collins's header.

Just as we're thinking WHU will do everything but score, the breakthrough comes. Mark Noble swings in an inviting cross and Antonio does really well to head the ball across the keeper and into the far corner of the goal. Bunn appears to think it's going wide as he barely moves. Phew. Mystic Matt has worked his magic on Antonio again.

We still struggle to get a second, with Cresswell going close and Noble shooting just wide. Payet is much more involved now. The game drifts as Nigel asks me to tell the bloke from the Treasury in front of us that Carlton Cole scored for Celtic against Stranraer. Meanwhile, having to drink soft drinks in the pub is clearly affecting Mystic Matt, who is texting, 'Bilić could substitute eight or nine of them. Song, Valencia and Kouyaté could all be hooked.' He's done it again. From a Villa corner, Valencia breaks and plays a perfect pass through to Kouyaté, who chips over the keeper to make it 2-0.

The Villa fans unveil a couple of anti-Lerner banners and we join in their chants of 'Sack the board, sack the board!' They've been pretty noisy for fans of a team that are doomed and deserve more than the rubbish season they've endured.

My man of the match is James Tomkins, for playing with thirteen stitches in his head. Tomka's taken a lot of batterings in games but never complains – though being a Basildon lad he might have learned his survival skills in the clubs of Bas Vegas. In addition, he's cultivating a really excellent Victorian villain's beard. He might just have a great career ahead of him in silent movies, or perhaps as an extra in *Poldark*.

After three very late substitutions from Slaven, we head to the Central, where Nigel is befriended by two angry cockney Villa fans raging at their defending for Kouyaté's goal. 'Story of our f**king season, mate…' Michael the Whovian has an anecdote about holding a pub door open for Steven Moffat as Nigel and Michael discuss David Cameron's problems over an in-out referendum and whether British teams will still be able to play in Europe after Brexit. I'm able to remark, 'It only took West Ham six games to Brexit Europe this season.'

Not a great game, but it's an important three points. A poor performance in the first half, but we've seen off a struggling team with ten men. We remain sixth. And on thirty-nine points, I think we're safe now…

A couple of days later my Facebook news feed reveals an interesting and very Gallic interview with Dimitri Payet on BT Sport. Dimitri, who seems to be gloriously French, speaks of his relationship with the fans in the language of love: 'It was very quick, after just a few months. They took the time to know me as I did them. It gave me a lot of confidence … I felt they trusted me and were showing it by supporting me all the time. Today I often say, it is a love story. It's the first time in my career I have a song with my name. For me it's a love story.' He describes being close to tears at the reception upon his return against Liverpool and says, 'I think it amplified even more my love story with the fans.'

I just hope that doesn't mean he'll be off to Man United in the summer. Not often you get that amount of *amour* from a load of sweaty blokes in the Bobby Moore Stand… *Je t'aime Dimitri.*

10

COME ON YOU IRONWORKS

MY SEARCH FOR WEST HAM UNITED'S SOUL HAS TAKEN me to Trinity Buoy Wharf, where the offices of Thames Ironworks once stood. The club that became West Ham was originally formed as Thames Ironworks FC in 1895, which is why West Ham are still referred to as 'The Irons' and a pair of crossed riveting hammers is used in the West Ham United badge.

The club was the creation of Thames Ironworks' owner Arnold Hills – an Oxford graduate and tea-total vegetarian – with some practical help from foreman Dave Taylor.

You do wonder what that grand old Victorian philanthropist Mr Hills, president of the London Vegetarian Society and a man with ties to the Temperance League, might have made of latter-day stars like Bobby Moore drinking in the Black Lion, Frank McAvennie dating page-three stunner Jenny Blyth and Andy Carroll moving in with *TOWIE*'s Billi Mucklow.

The football club was presumably intended as a way of improving the moral fibre of the workforce and keeping the men away from pubs, women and fast horses and carts. Thames Ironworks initially played at grounds in Hermit Road in Canning Town and Browning Road in East Ham and then the Memorial Grounds in West Ham in 1897. In 1900, Thames Ironworks FC became West Ham United and moved to the Boleyn Ground in 1904. Even the earliest games against the rival dockers of Millwall sparked trouble.

The main shipbuilding yard once stood across the mouth of the River Lea, in an area that is now fairly inaccessible to the pedestrian, so Trinity Buoy Wharf, which housed the offices of the Thames Ironworks, is the best place to get a view of the peninsula where the Ironworks factory stood and also the slipway, where huge battleships were launched into the Thames.

Trinity Buoy Wharf is a fascinating place. Much of Canning Town now looks like Hong Kong, with tower blocks being erected amid concrete flyovers. But here at Leamouth, on this once-boggy peninsula on the Thames, stand the Victorian buildings and a lighthouse.

The wharf is a short walk from East India DLR station. It was once used to build maritime buoys and test lighthouses. Now it's home to bohemians and hipsters, an artistic community with studios in old shipping containers, all stacked on top of each other. Across the choppy grey waters of the Thames stands the dome of the O2 Arena. By the riverside, there's an unlikely piece of chrome-clad Americana in Fat Boy's Diner. We visit the homely Bow Creek Café, a converted container, which offers wooden seats outside amid thyme plants, fairy lights and sculptures by the creek. The all-day breakfast is great. It could easily be in San Francisco were it just a little sunnier. And it's now so middle-class that we bump into a couple from Stoke Newington whose son used to go to the same nursery as my oldest daughter. They plan to walk back to Stokey via the River Lea, they tell us.

We look across the mouth of Bow Creek towards the site of the Italianate factory of Thames Ironworks. Now the stretch of land on which the Ironworks once stood is home to the warehouses of ASD Metal Services. So maybe there is still some connection with iron on the site.

There's a noticeboard on the wharfside detailing the history of the Thames Ironworks, with pictures of huge warships being launched into the Thames. It would once have employed 3,000 men and been alive with bustle and clanging hammers. The Ironworks launched 120 massive ships into the Thames, including the HMS *Warrior* in 1860 and HMS *Thunderer* in 1912.

Three years after the football club was formed, in 1898, the launch of the battleship HMS *Albion* created a huge wave that overwhelmed a pontoon and swept thirty-seven people to their deaths. On YouTube there's old footage of the massive ship entering the water, surrounded by boats full of onlookers and massive crowds on the quays, and some very moving pictures of the confused aftermath of the disaster.

Walk to the nearby East London Cemetery at Plaistow and amid the tombstones you'll find a sad memorial of an anchor from the HMS *Albion* and the names and ages of the victims.

Recently, bits of the old ironworks have been re-discovered. During the Crossrail excavations of 2012, the old Thames Ironworks slipway was discovered on the Limmo Peninsula along with the floor of the foundry and furnace, machine bases with bolts and a railway (but no sign of West Ham's trophy cabinet).

Near to where we are standing, in Orchard Place, were the offices, model shop and joiners shop of Thames Ironworks. A chain-ferry linked the two sides of the creek. At the main Ironworks were the dry docks, rolling mills, furnaces and plating and engineering shops.

So much of London is layers of history and it's not hard to step back a century to the days when the fiercely moustached Ironworks side played the likes of Crouch End FC. Their fans would have been hard-working men from tight communities, who had to trek to Poplar for basic provisions. The history boards on the old warehouse walls in Orchard Place reveal the area used to be known as Bog Island. The community was populated by three main families. In the late nineteenth century, the school had 160 children, of whom a hundred had the same surname of Lammin.

In the 1890s, the local priest, Father Lawless, described the locals as 'Hardly human … incarnate mushrooms … God must have made a mistake making them.' No, that was Millwall fans, surely?

Initially it would have been a trek down Manor Road to watch the Irons play at the Memorial Grounds. When the football club moved to the Boleyn the local fans would have had to walk to Canning Town and along the Barking Road to Upton Park.

As well as building and maintaining buoys, the wharf's other job was testing lighthouses. One of the lightships built by Thames Ironworks has been restored as a recording studio and is moored behind Fat Boy's Diner. At the end of the wharf is a brick lighthouse. We ascend the stairs and read notices about how 'Longplayer', a piece of never-ending music, has been playing in the lighthouse since 2000. It's not 'Billy Bonds' Claret and Blue Army' or 'Bubbles', but something more ethereal. Bizarrely, it was composed by Jem Finer of the Pogues.

Set in the former lamp room, 'Longplayer' uses the sounds of Tibetan 'singing bowls' (which are not unlike metal dog bowls) to take us 'on an atmospheric journey into time and space'. The music is a series of weird sounds rather like some *Doctor Who* soundtrack. We gaze through the round window at the beautiful vista of the meandering Thames and watch a flock of seagulls swoop over the warehouses, as if dancing in a slow ballet to the music.

Heading back down Orchard Place, Nell takes some display pictures for her dad, giving me the 'Tumblr look'. The road is full of artworks. I stand beneath a giant fish strung between warehouses, by a graffiti letter P, before some arty, dock-inspired pictures and a giant woman's face with huge eyes. Then by a London taxi with a tree growing out of the roof.

My family head home, but I decide to explore the peninsula where the main Thames Ironworks' factory stood. It's the most pedestrian-hostile area in London. From the bunker of Canning Town station there's a concrete flyover called the Silvertown Viaduct with a lonely pavement. Every other vehicle is a giant cement lorry. The vista is cranes, pylons, building sites, new tower blocks, low-flying aircraft from the City Airport and, to give it all a *Blade Runner*-style futuristic sheen, the suspended pod cars of the London Gondola gliding through the sky.

I descend a set of concrete steps that smell of urine and cross a roundabout where the passing lorries create dust clouds. Dock Road takes me into a *Sweeney*-esque landscape, past giant discarded tyres on verges and on to warehouses where skips are piled high and machines tear apart scrap metal. Scarab Close is similarly bleak and ends in private warehouses and signs reading 'authorized persons only'. Somewhere under this industrial hinterland lies the original Thames Ironworks, but as huge trucks pass and the pavement turns to mud it feels dangerous to explore further lest this fan becomes buried with the Ironworks too.

I trek back over the Lower Lea Crossing, where you can view the sweep of the river from the flyover and see some mud and bulrushes on the banks. The only other pedestrian is an Eastern European construction worker. There's an ecology centre on the Limmo Peninsula, while the other Peninsula is a mini-Manhattan called Island City.

My final stop of the day is a trek down Manor Road, which runs parallel to the Jubilee Line, to the Memorial Recreation Grounds at West Ham. This was where West Ham played before moving to the Boleyn Stadium.

The Memorial was created as a grand, philanthropic gesture by Arnold Hills, who bought the land and had the grounds built in six months. They opened on 22 June 1897, on the sixtieth anniversary of Queen Victoria's coronation, and were pretty grand for the time. The football pitch was in the middle of a banked cycling track – a sort of Victorian Velodrome (and not dissimilar to the bowl of the Olympic Stadium). There was also an athletics track, a posh new stand and one of the largest outdoor swimming pools in the country.

Early Hammers games attracted crowds of 2,000 and in a few pictures of matches the fans can be seen grouped on top of the banked cycle track and behind the goals. The football ground was even used to host a boxing match in 1909. Arnold Hills employed his influence to get West Ham station built in 1901, but even with this the gates were still relatively disappointing, and with Hills unwilling to renew the lease, the club moved to the Boleyn in 1904 and finally attracted bigger crowds.

From Memorial Avenue I enter the Memorial Recreation Grounds, going past modern changing rooms that are faced with lumps of rock set behind mesh, to deter the local graffiti artists. Looking at the old plans of the Recreation Grounds, it seems that West Ham would have played in the northern corner of the park by the District Line, with the East London Cemetery border fence to its east. Today there's still a pitch, though it's the home of the East London Rugby Club, who have a rather grand-looking club house.

There are also some AstroTurf pitches behind wire mesh and a couple of proper old-fashioned football pitches with green grass by the border with the East London Cemetery. A couple of British Asian lads kick a football about on the grass and a few school kids play on swings, but mid-afternoon in February there's not too much life, though there's a *Teletubbies*-style sunken building with a grass roof that houses a café. Arnold Hills would be delighted that it is still being used as a community sports ground.

In the centre of the park, there's a sculpture by Theresa Smith commemorating both Thames Ironworks FC and the *Albion* disaster. It was commissioned by West Ham and Plaistow New Deal for Communities.

Smith's sculpture takes the form of eleven metal posts laid out in the shape of the hull of HMS *Albion*, but also representing West Ham's eleven players. Attached to each metal rib is a shipworker's hammer. It all works rather well. Looking through some of the steel ribs, you can see the new London of Canary Wharf and regenerated Docklands.

A rusting sign explains that the sculpture is a memorial to the football club, the Ironworks and the thirty-eight victims of the HMS *Albion* disaster who are buried in the adjoining cemetery. It continues:

> This work is a memorial to those victims but also marks a once great local industry and the craft of its workers, bringing back the clang of hammer on steel. The sound of the riveting gangs of the Thames Ironworks is gone forever but the heritage is still celebrated today in the fans' chant: 'Come on you Irons!'

It's not too difficult to imagine the hardened steelworkers trekking across the Memorial to watch the Irons in a rare moment of relaxation. The smells of refreshments, the good humour, hubbub and ferment would probably have been the same as at a lower-league game today.

There's much to reflect on seeing West Ham's old ground and it's a reminder that this won't be the first time we've moved. Perhaps in 100 years' time, when West Ham leave the Olympic Stadium to move to a giant stadium 40,000 feet up in the sky – rather like Cloudbase, the headquarters of Spectrum in *Captain Scarlet* – there will be fans getting tearful about their last visit to Westfield. History is beneath our feet in London, and West Ham will surely carry on as a repository of workers' dreams wherever the team plays.

11

TOTTENHAM HOTSPUR – IT'S HAPPENED AGAIN!

IS THIS WEST HAM'S POST-CHRISTMAS SLUMP ARRIVING in early February? The Irons lose 1-0 at ten-man Southampton in a midweek match. Last season, West Ham were fourth at Christmas under Sam Allardyce but then faded to finish twelfth, which explains the nervousness of some fans.

The Saints go ahead after nine minutes, when Yoshida pokes home a cross from close range, after Enner Valencia has inadvertently knocked the ball into his path. Saints' keeper Fraser Forster has to make a great save from Winston Reid's header, but that's the Irons' best chance.

When Wanyama is red-carded for lunging at Payet, it seems we'll surely equalise. Slaven brings on two strikers in Carroll and new loan signing Emenike, and Emenike has a header wide of the post with his first touch. But we don't really threaten after that. The Saints twice go close on the break. A late Owen Farrell-style free kick from Enner Valencia is dubbed 'the worst free kick of all time!' in Matt's irate text from the pub. Though Southampton have now kept five clean sheets in a row since the return of Forster, and it was never an easy game.

However, any doubts about the way our season might be going disappear in the FA Cup replay against Liverpool. I have to miss the match as it clashes with my daughter Nell's fifteenth birthday and she wants us to go for a family dinner. And just occasionally I have to remember that family comes before football. We celebrate in Byron with a burger and a Punk IPA for Dad.

Back at home, I catch the latter stages on the radio. It's a superb atmosphere at the Boleyn as the radio commentator gets involved in a not-very-PC metaphor for the ground: 'The old girl bats her eyelids and shows she can still do it.'

Early in the match, Coutinho hits the woodwork for Jürgen Klopp's men and goal machine Joey O'Brien, in at right-back, has a shot deflected against the post for the Irons. Payet strikes the post with another superb free kick and from the rebound Mignolet makes a sharp save to deny Kouyaté's header. It's riveting stuff.

West Ham take the lead just before the break as Payet finds Valencia and Enner's fine cross sits up for Antonio to score with a controlled, van Basten-style volley. Unexpected and a piece of footballing mastery from Michail.

However, early in the second half, Liverpool win a free kick. West Ham's wall jumps over the ball and Coutinho scores with a low drive. Randolph looks slow to react too.

Winston Reid pulls a hamstring and late in the game the curse of the right-backs strikes Joey O'Brien, who limps off to be replaced by Moses.

Text reports reach me from Upton Park claiming that Matt is struggling to stay positive. Nigel suggests that Lisa needs to take him back to San Francisco quickly. Antonio has a lobbed effort tipped over and West Ham should be awarded a penalty when Valencia is pulled back by Ilori as he goes for Antonio's cross. Randolph has to save Benteke's free kick and Ibe's long-range effort before the ninety minutes is up with the score 1-1. Matt texts: 'When a series of shite corners ends with nowt but Reid out for the rest of the season I am being tested. Extra time in the FA Cup against Liverpool. What could possibly go wrong?'

So it's into extra time, with Antonio as an emergency right-back and Kouyaté off after being knocked out in a worrying clash of heads. Noble has a decent effort saved by Mignolet and the hapless Benteke misses with a volley and then loses a one-on-one duel with Randolph. Sturridge shoots just over the top as the Scousers finish strongly and might well win it.

It looks certain to go to penalties until the last minute of extra time, when Lucas gives away a silly free kick on the right flank with a push on Valencia. Payet curls in a geometrically perfect cross and Ogbonna rises brilliantly to thump home a Carroll-esque header. Upton Park goes barmy as Oggy runs to the Chicken Run and is buried under a mound of players.

The Hammers fans are chanting 'Que sera, sera, whatever will be will be, we're going to Wem-ber-ley.' Matt texts, 'Oggy Oggy Oggy, oi oi oi!' Some unlikely heroes tonight in Oggy, O'Brien, Antonio and Randolph.

If this is the final Cup tie at the Boleyn, then it's a fitting finish. So that's three wins in a season over Liverpool and an aggregate score of 7-1. A graphic of the 7-1 score over four matches (3-0, 2-0, 0-0 and 2-1) goes round the Facebook groups. Could this be our year for saying goodbye to the Boleyn with a Cup win? Since we last won a major trophy in 1980, teams such as Portsmouth have won the FA Cup and Swansea City and Oxford United the League Cup. Surely we're due our turn?

Slaven Bilić's comments after the Liverpool match prove he knows exactly what West Ham fans want. Bilić says: 'It is a special night. Yes, tomorrow is a new day and we have to concentrate on Norwich tomorrow, but tonight there is no harm at all in saying this is a special night for our club. I'm so proud and happy for my players and proud of everyone that has any connection with the club because it is a great night for West Ham. OK, it is only for the last sixteen but it was a late night kick-off, it was against Liverpool, it's our last season at Upton Park, it's over 120 minutes and we scored with a great header in the last second of the game despite having injuries. We overcame all of that so that is why this game will go down as one of the greatest nights and games in West Ham's history.'

Yes, he exaggerates a little, but he speaks of emotion, pride, heart and special nights. In many ways, the winning goal was straight from the Big Sam textbook; a set-piece and a thumping header. But, whereas Allardyce would have spoken pragmatically about grinding out a result, Bilić appears to get what being a fan is all about and realises that there's always something romantic about a win under the lights in E13.

That great result against Liverpool is followed by more good news (unless you're the club's accountants). Dimitri Payet has signed an improved five-year contract on a rumoured £120,000 a week. There have been rumours of several clubs sniffing around Dimitri, including a mystery Chinese club, Man City and Chelsea. So at least Dimitri should now be able to afford the petrol for his ostentatious yellow Lamborghini, which can be seen parked in the players' car park.

West Ham have had to up his wages, but if any one player is going to fill the Olympic Stadium, it's Payet. He's very much our talisman and it's a big signal to keep him for next season and hopefully the rest of his career. David Sullivan has said Payet's the best player he's ever signed. Presumably the fans' song was crucial in Payet's decision. Unless our rival fans can find a better Billy Ray Cyrus tune, hopefully we've got Dimitri married to the claret-and-blue cause.

My old pal Shane Barber, former editor of *On A Mission From God* fanzine, calls it right when he comments: 'The really good part is two-fold; firstly, the cringeworthy video that tugs at the heartstrings, but good luck to them. Secondly, the fact that the new deal will undoubtedly be tied to a huge buyout number if anyone else wants to sign him. If we have a number around £80 million, that should be enough to put off even the most avaricious clubs. Sully's no mug; we'll be well covered. Let's be honest, every club needs one star that lights their firmament; Dimi's ours. The only downside is if he gets injured, his part has been talked up so much that the rest don't think they can perform without him.'

Further evidence that West Ham have a side of some character emerging comes four days after the bruising encounter with Liverpool as the Irons fight back from two goals down to draw at Norwich. West Ham score in the seventy-fourth and seventy-sixth minutes, which isn't bad after playing 120 minutes against Liverpool on Tuesday.

West Ham's comeback begins when substitute Victor Moses makes a determined run from the half-way line and, despite being tackled, gets a shot in; Payet strokes home the rebound after Moses's effort is blocked. The other substitute, Andy Carroll, returning after his injury at Bournemouth, does well to find Payet on the left. From Dimitri's cut-back Mark Noble thumps home from the edge of the box with a shot that makes the net billow. He wheels away in delight; Nobes deserves a goal because he's been playing really well of late.

At the end it could have gone either way, with Norwich poking wide a good chance and Emenike just falling to get a decent connection with an inviting cross.

West Ham now have forty points by 13 February – we're safe! That is, unless someone goes down on forty-two points, as West Ham did in 2002–03, setting a record points total for a relegated team.

The following Sunday sees the FA Cup tie at Blackburn televised live. It's off to the Heeltap at London Bridge to watch the game with coffee-drinking Lisa and Matt (both preparing for shifts) and Michael the Whovian. Matt's wearing his lucky Botafogo shirt, as you do.

On twenty minutes, Blackburn take the lead as Antonio turns his back on the ball and Marshall drills a low shot into the corner, deceiving our Cup keeper Darren Randolph.

Thankfully we're up against a struggling Championship side. The Rovers' midfield parts to allow Moses to run at their defence and he fires in a low shot that goes straight through Jason Steele (whom, as Matt says, sounds like a 1970s superhero).

The Gav arrives with the score at 1-1 and orders a pint of Spitfire. He brings us good fortune as Taylor fouls Moses thirty yards out and Dimitri Payet curls a sumptuous free kick into the top corner. He makes it looks easy. Lover-man Dimitri runs into the arms of Super Slaven.

Ten minutes into the second half, Rovers' Taylor stupidly fouls Moses and receives a second yellow, so we're up against ten men. At this point we force Matt to say that Emenike will never score for the Hammers. It works superbly. Emergency right-back Antonio, playing as a virtual winger, gets a shot in that's blocked; in the ensuing melee Kouyaté pulls the ball across the box for Emenike to prod home.

'Mystic Matt!' we cry.

Emenike hits the post when he should score and the Irons have a series of goals disallowed for offside. But there's a wobble at 3-1 as Kouyaté is red-carded; he's unlucky to be sent off for clipping Rovers' Henley on the edge of the box. The contact looked minimal and the ball wasn't under Henley's control. (Kouyaté's red card is later rescinded.)

The imperious Payet decides to finish the game off, playing in Emenike, who rounds the keeper to stroke home his second. Two minutes into added time, Payet glides from his own half as if he's the footballing equivalent of a yellow Lamborghini. He takes on what seems like the entire Rovers' side and scores a stunning fifth from the edge of the box. Seven thousand Hammers fans celebrate wildly in the away section. It's a long time since we've scored five on the road.

We wonder again if it's going to be our year for the Cup and if the Heeltap is our new lucky pub. Meanwhile, Gav reminisces about the difficulties of finding a Zenit Saint Petersburg handbook in -21°C Russia. A great result. So now it's Shrewsbury away in the quarter-finals – that is, unless their opponents, struggling Man United, pull off a giant-killing.

After the match, Slaven Bilić is positively Byronic in his praise for Payet. 'I have to get poetry lessons to describe his importance to us,' he gushes. It's not often that West Ham and poetry are mentioned in the same sentence, though that William Shakespeare did knock off a few sonnets in Stratford. And it's possible that W. H. Auden's 'Stop All the Clocks' was a reference to the dodgy scoreboards at the Boleyn.

It's hard to imagine Sam Allardyce being so poetic; and the return of Big Sam to Upton Park with his Sunderland side preoccupies the *Evening Standard*, with Sam, never slow to promote himself, claiming, 'I saved a broken West Ham.' In footballing terms, he has a point, though the problem was that, in PR terms, Allardyce, whose take-it-or-leave-it gruff persona might suit some northern underdog clubs, was never right for West Ham, where the descendants of hardened ironworkers still want a little fantasy and escapism. Saying that he didn't know what the West Ham way was got him off to a terrible start and the low point was cupping his ear to the fans after the unconvincing win against ten-man Hull.

But it's also fair to say that, despite some West Ham fans refusing to admit that anything he ever did was of any value, Sam did save the club from going the way of relegated clubs like Bolton, Wigan and Leeds. It's very difficult to get promoted first time and Allardyce achieved that despite having to revamp the entire squad, giving us a great day at Wembley in the process. It wasn't always pretty but the finishes of tenth, fourteenth and twelfth established the club back in the

Premier League – though the post-Christmas fade last season suggested the time was right to change for both parties.

He made some unsuccessful buys, like Matt Jarvis, but it was also on Allardyce's watch that the core of the current side arrived, such as Adrián, Cresswell, Collins, Kouyaté, Song, Carroll, Valencia and Sakho. He also coached Winston Reid and James Tomkins into becoming much better players. Team spirit was good. The players seemed to enjoy playing for Allardyce and at times his long-ball reputation was exaggerated. Mark Noble would not have kept his place if the team was an exclusively long-ball outfit and we still score a lot of headers from crosses now, without any criticism of Bilić.

So I won't be joining in the boos aimed at Big Sam, though the time was right for both parties to part. Slaven Bilić is much better at saying what the fans want to hear and he suits our club. He understands the fans' need for entertainment and glory nights. We could do without Sam yet again saying how over-demanding West Ham fans are, but Allardyce does deserve some credit for being part of that building process too.

On match day, the big news in Ken's Café is that Nigel's doing warm weather training in Dubai, so Lisa has his ticket, and Matt's met a barber who knows even more stats than he does. There's a huge queue outside the café, due to the 12.45 p.m. kick-off. Michael the Whovian is way behind us with his big breakfast order. I'm with my younger daughter Nell, who's worried we won't get a table, but I explain that it's an immutable law of Ken's that a table always materialises, as indeed one does.

During our long wait for food we wonder if the venerable Fraser was at the 8-0 Sunderland match back in 1968. 'Fraser would have been saying that Greenwood should resign as he only played four forwards,' quips Matt.

Our food arrives at 12.40 p.m. 'I don't care what they say about you, Carol, I think you do a fantastic job!' says Mike, as Carol explains the vagaries of ticket-hunting fans and early kick-offs and tells him not to be cheeky.

Nell's impressed by the speed I manage to eat my eggs, chips and beans, so I explain that you can do anything with a kick-off as an incentive: 'Treat everything in life as if you're going to miss the kick-off and you won't go wrong.' My aphorism certainly appeals to Michael, who has moved to a separate table to begin demolition work on his big breakfast.

We arrive five minutes after kick-off, but haven't missed much. I'm in Nell's seat, which is in the back of Row R in the corner, where you can't even see the non-working scoreboard. Fraser says Big Sam was greeted by indifference, with the crowd's ire reserved for Defoe. We think Sam might have been tempted to sign Paul Ince and Frank Lampard as human shields for this one.

Sunderland are more difficult to beat now they've signed Koné, Kirchhoff, Khazri and N'Doye. The game's a scrappy affair, with the crowd quiet after rushing their lunches. Khazri almost scores after some poor control by Adrián and then hits the top of the bar with a fine dipping free kick. In turn, Noble, set up by Lanzini, has a thunderous shot tipped onto the bar by Mannone. You wish Nobes would try that more.

We take the lead when Antonio wriggles through two defenders into the box and passes a curling shot into the far corner. A great effort and his fifth of the season. Michail celebrates with a bizarre Homer Simpson 'grass dancing' routine on the turf, lying down and wiggling his legs in demented fashion. As silly goal celebrations go, it's up there with Frank Lampard's run around the corner flag, Kevin Nolan's clucking chicken and the late Eamonn Dolan's Irish jig.

'Down with Johnson! You're going down with Johnson!' chant the Bobby Moore Stand, mindful of the ex-Sunderland winger's current court case and sacking by the club after admitting a charge of sexual activity with a fifteen-year-old girl.

Antonio has a snap-shot saved by Mannone and then it's half-time. We ponder making changes. 'You don't want Carroll to come on against Sunderland because he'll try too hard and get injured,' says Matt. 'Or Liverpool, because he used to play for them, or Newcastle.'

'Or anyone, really,' I add.

Michael makes a determined sortie to accost Irons-supporting actor Donald Sumpter, Lord High President of the Time Lords. He's not interested in an interview with Michael's friend Toby, but is available for read-throughs, says Sumpter, so a bit of a result for our budding playwright.

The second half sees West Ham start slowly and Sunderland create chances. Defoe volleys wide and Adrián makes a great save from sub Rodwell. Andy Carroll comes on for Emenike and runs around like a loose horse at the Grand National. He unsettles the Mackems' defence, though he should probably score when he volleys (or, looking at the replay, actually shins) Byram's knock-down onto the bar. Cresswell gets into the box twice, only to fall over. But we see the match out thanks to good games from Ogbonna and Collins and a great late tackle from Byram that denies Rodwell.

'Twist and Shout' and 'Highway to Hell' are on the PA after the final whistle as I try to extricate myself from the back of the stand. Not a great game, but we go up to fifth. 'It was a bit like a Big Sam tribute game, really – a scrappy 1-0 win,' suggests Matt as we head to the Central. I ask Nell if there was any swearing, because Matt really doesn't approve of bad language, being a vicar's son.

Big Sam is all over the BT screen, saying that Sunderland just need to be more clinical in front of goal. We've heard that before. But it's West Ham who have respected the three points. And we're definitely safe on forty-three points now.

Four days later comes our last-ever game at the Boleyn against Spurs.

There's another big queue in Ken's Café, but Lisa and myself get our orders in by 6.30 p.m. hoping to avoid another missed kick-off. A bloke sitting at our table says that he's been coming to Ken's since 1979 and wonders when it first opened. I'm able to tell him that, according to the newly discovered Ken's Café Facebook page, it's been going for forty-nine years, since 1967. We then discuss the absurdity of selling half-and-half scarves for this game, wondering if they do a Millwall/West Ham one.

Michael the Renaissance Fan arrives carrying a Rough Trade bag containing *X-Ray Audio*, a book about Russian music fans who made bootlegs on X-ray plates. 'Bit of a niche market that,' I suggest. Michael's big breakfast arrives suspiciously quickly and we suspect that he might finally have qualified for VIP treatment from Carol.

Then there's a late appearance from Nigel, back from

his warm weather training in Dubai, where he managed to see Toto live. He also announces that he's watched the Metropolitan Police play at Imber Court, where they presumably got out of jail after some criminal defending.

We try to get to the East Stand, only to be turned away by riot police at the end of Tudor Road. It all seems a bit over the top, with the Moore, Hurst and Peters statue being boarded up and police vans all the way up an unnecessarily congested Green Street. Even Fraser misses the kick-off for the first time in living memory.

But inside the Boleyn it's a cracking atmosphere, as chants of 'Bubbles', 'Come on you Irons!', 'Who are yer!' and 'Lasagne … whoooah!' ring out in the riotous football theatre of E13.

West Ham score after just seven minutes. Lanzini forces a corner. From Payet's kick Antonio loses Chadli to head in off the post, with Lloris slow to react. Michail runs to the Chicken Run and does another strange skipping and dancing routine – apparently the Carlton Dance from *The Fresh Prince of Bel-Air* – as Upton Park erupts. A big throaty roar of 'Who are yer! Who are yer!' taunts the Spurs fans.

'This is almost as good as watching the Metropolitan Police,' suggests Nigel.

It's Antonio's sixth goal of the season. If Payet wasn't certain to win the Hammer of the Year contest, he'd now be a contender. You can feel the hunger every time he plays;

Antonio chases back to surge into tackles and celebrates goals like they're still a novelty.

He's certainly had to work for his career, starting off at Tooting and Mitcham, then signing for Reading, where he had loan spells at Tooting again, Cheltenham, Southampton and Colchester. After signing for Sheffield Wednesday, he moved on to Nottingham Forest, where he became a big hit with the fans, before moving to the Hammers for £7 million.

He didn't complain when he wasn't in the team and since breaking into the side has shown work rate and real skill, such as the cushioned volley against Liverpool and that mazy dribble and curled finish against Sunderland. He's still just twenty-five and Antonio is surely a player who can only get better.

It's a really impressive first half from West Ham. Bilić has made a clever tactical tweak, playing Kouyaté in the back three with Antonio and Cresswell as wing-backs. The team work immensely hard and out-press Tottenham. The hard-working Emenike closes down Lloris and almost forces an error. Noble has another long-range humdinger pushed wide and only a desperate tackle denies Antonio. Emenike works the channels well, with Wimmer booked for bringing him down.

We're a bit mystified as to what to complain about at half-time, though Nigel, munching a lucky smoked salmon bagel, counsels caution, as Spurs will surely improve in the second half.

Indeed, Spurs start brightly with Adrián having to parry Alderweireld's long-range effort and Kane missing the rebound. Eriksen then cuts in from the right to force another save from the Hammers' custodian. But we retain our work rate, with Obiang and Noble excelling in midfield and Antonio never stopping running. Emenike is brought down by Wimmer, when he appears about to shoot, and the crowd demands a red card. Instead, the ref awards a free kick to Spurs. Good job Matt, away working on the Dr Feelgood-style night shift, wasn't here to see that. 'Fie on your face, referee! A pox on you!' suggests Michael, our resident Shakespearian.

Antonio prods a Payet free kick over the bar, before James Collins has to go off injured to be replaced by young Reece Oxford. A big test for the youngster in the last twenty-five minutes, but he's assured throughout.

'It's happened again, it's happened again, Tottenham Hotspur, it's happened again...' chant the West Ham fans.

We're getting Sakho in the evening as Diafra replaces Lanzini and Andy Carroll comes on for Emenike. Harry Kane slashes a cross wide, to the derision of the home fans, as cries of 'SUPER SUPER SLAV! SUPER SLAVEN BILIĆ!' fill Upton Park.

There's four minutes of added time as Cresswell shoots over and the Bobby Moore Stand break into a rousing, and accurate, chant of 'F**k all! You're gonna win f**k all!'

Sakho runs it into the corners, which he's good at, and buys more time.

The whistle blows to huge acclaim as Slaven's men leave the pitch. That's our last-ever Upton Park win against Spurs and it's been some night. 'So we're making a late bid for the title?' suggests Fraser. And we're definitely safe now on forty-six points…

We retreat to the Central, where the barmaid is baffled by a request for Old Speckled Hen, at first thinking it's cider. We're joined by Nigel's chastened Spurs-supporting former boss Andy and his son Tom. Michael suggests that standards are dropping at the Central as there's no woman selling dodgy DVDs and no clearing the tables early for backpackers' breakfasts. Nigel offers support for this by saying he's discovered soap in the Gents. But we're so happy we can cope with anything. Meanwhile, the TV provides astonishing proof that we're only one point off fourth spot.

As we leave the Central and traipse past the illuminated stands of the Boleyn, Fraser lights a celebratory cigar. The empty stands dominating the skyline look particularly romantic when viewed from that angle on the Barking Road. It's our last victory at home against Spurs. Tottenham Hotspur, it's happened again…

It's three games in a week for the Hammers as the following Saturday we take on Everton. It's a ground we never win at and an initially depressing listen on the radio. Lukaku, who always scores against us, gives Everton the lead after rolling Oxford and firing in off the post. Everton's Mirallas is sent off for two bookings, but even so WHU go two goals down after some good link play between Lukaku and goal-scorer Aaron Lennon.

It looks like a thrashing as ten-man Everton get a penalty, even though Song's foul was outside the box. But Lukaku's tame effort is saved by Adrián, while the Hammers' keeper then prevents another goal in a one-on-one with Lukaku. It could easily be 4-0.

I text Matt: 'Need some Payet magic now. Not optimistic with no defenders though.'

Matt texts back: 'No chance whatsoever.'

Bilić has made changes, bringing on strikers Carroll and Sakho in the second half. Big Andy immediately causes panic in the Everton defence. With twelve minutes to go Antonio heads home Noble's cross to give the Hammers a consolation.

But, incredibly, three minutes later, Payet crosses for Sakho to get between two defenders and head home. We're on for a very unlikely point.

The game moves into added time. With ninety minutes gone, Cresswell crosses from deep, Carroll heads down, Sakho produces a great back flick and Payet anticipates to strike home. Football, bloody hell.

We survive six minutes of added time to earn a fantastic win and go fifth, one point behind Man City.

Matt texts: 'Just to clarify I meant Everton had no chance whatsoever at 2-0 up and with Lukaku taking a penalty. Obvs.'

And then Big Joe sends a message from the away end: 'According to 2,999 gentlemen (and ladies) next to me, We've got Payet!'

I sit open-mouthed before my Apple Mac. When was the last time West Ham came from 2-0 down to win 3-2 away from home? Or won away to Liverpool and Everton in the same season? Or scored three goals in twelve minutes? This team might be something special.

That week I start to dream about what 'We've got Payet!' might sound like sung at Wembley as we go 3-0 up in the FA Cup Final. Or what the celebrations might be like if West Ham gate-crashed the Champions League. And if Leicester City are still top of the league anything can happen.

But that way madness lies. This is West Ham. Just think ahead to the next game. Fortune will hide at some point, it always does.

12

MORE BOOKINGS AT THE NEWHAM BOOKSHOP

THE NEWHAM BOOKSHOP IS THE BEST INDEPENDENT bookshop in London and a pre-match institution for many West Ham fans. It's distinctive yellow sign sits in Barking Road opposite the statue of West Ham's World Cup winners. The windows are full of posters advertising everything from Harper Lee's *Go Set a Watchman* to *People of the Abyss* and the latest West Ham offerings.

At the counter the teetering piles of books give it a pleasingly Dickensian feel and manager Vivian Archer is a one-woman literary encyclopaedia. Flyers advertise a never-ending series of literary events and talks. It's a salon for the soccerati before West Ham games and my daughters, when they were younger, used to love the children's section. It veers from high politics to local history, via football, fiction, horror, humour, hooliology and cups of tea for the favoured.

Over the years, the Newham Bookshop has hosted every conceivable West Ham signing. 'The biggest signing was John Lyall just after they failed to renew his contract,' recalls Vivian. 'They were hanging off the ceiling and he was a really nice man. Trevor Brooking spoke to everybody. Jimmy Greaves was lovely, but we had more Spurs fans than West Ham. The most unusual was Frank McAvennie before a Millwall game on a Sunday. He was a little late as he'd been out the night before, but it was a good signing even if it was a bit hairy because it was Millwall.'

The Newham Bookshop itself was set up by a group of parents in 1978 and is still a non-profit organisation. Archer has been managing the shop for twenty-eight years, having previously worked as an actress in the 1970s, including TV work on the likes of *Z-Cars*. 'I decided I didn't want to be out of work and someone in Hackney said "Can you help in a bookshop?" and that was it. I'd always loved reading and loved talking to people so then I started working here. I couldn't work in any other environment now. I have complete control over what I order. We do events most nights. I could have retired a while ago, but I love doing it.'

My own signings at the bookshop – for *Hammers in the Heart*, *West Ham: Irons in the Soul* and *The Joy of Essex* – involved sitting at a table on the Barking Road or at the back of the shop. Not many writers get their own table. We'd try to entice match-day punters to our tomes and quite often fans would compliment me on my blog. You get personal feedback here: Vivian told me about one customer who bought seven copies of *The Joy of Essex*, a personal career high. She also revealed that a scaffolder who hadn't read a book in thirty years bought *Irons in the Soul* from her shop. You don't get that at Waterstones.

The regular Christmas shopping evenings were unlikely literary salons. I'd be chatting over mince pies to Cass Pennant about West Ham and then discussing poetry with Benjamin Zephaniah, a long-time supporter of the shop. The late Gilda O'Neill was a lovely woman who wrote tales of her childhood in the East End, while I also befriended crime writer Barbara Nadel at these soirées, along with numerous other local writers and shop supporters.

Vivian's also had me selling books at stalls at Columbia Road Flower Market, the Redbridge Green Fair, the East London History Fair and Stratford Theatre.

Archer's style was described aptly by writer and Biteback publisher Iain Dale in the bookshop's thirty-fifth anniversary booklet:

> Vivian greets every customer that walks through the door, always seems to know where the book they're looking for is, and there's usually a recommendation to come with it. This isn't just the lost art of customer service, but a commitment to her community which can also be seen from the events Newham Bookshop participate in, to people doing work experience in the shop.

Indeed, she's a difficult woman to interview, as while we speak she's constantly stopping to chat with locals and to direct customers to books.

Other West Ham-related signings that Vivian has organised over the years include Geoff Hurst, Martin Peters, Danny Dyer, Steve Bacon, Brian Williams, Jeremy Nicholas, Robert Banks, Iain Dale, Cass Pennant, Tina Moore and Brian Belton. The Cockney Rejects 'were great, really nice guys, and big anti-racist campaigners'.

The shop has never been scared to stock tales from the days of football violence. Books by the likes of Cass Pennant and Bill Gardner can be seen mingling with high politics, philosophy and sociological tomes. 'Cass's book tells a really good story and he can write well. Writers like Cass feel comfortable in here. If you're a local bookshop you have to make it welcoming to everybody,' says Archer.

The players tend not to be book browsers, 'but Robert

Green's mum came in saying "My son's just having his medical." She bought some quite literary titles.'

Actor Terence Stamp was once a regular, Phill Jupitus comes in and Russell Brand has been spotted too. But there's been no sign of Super Slaven yet, says Vivian, though former West Ham chairman Terry Brown used to buy a lot of books on local history and 'the Icelandic guy and his wife bought a lot of books'.

A lot of overseas supporters frequent the bookshop too. 'We've had the Belgian Irons all coming in off their coach, Swedes, Norwegians and a lot of Australians... They email and I order a load of books for them.'

Hopefully the Newham Bookshop, where Archer's colleague John Newman runs a great children's section, will continue to prosper even after the stadium move, as it knows its customers so well.

'We'll miss the Saturdays, but we don't rely on football – it's a bonus. We'll have to see who moves into the new flats, too,' says Archer.

Her successful formula for the shop is simple: 'Know your audience and listen to them. When the reps come in I can say I'll buy one of these for a customer who likes books on buses from the 1950s or volume three of the history of Romford FC. The bookshop listens to people and reflects the area with all the diversity and changes. The dictionaries tell us who's moving in. We used to sell a lot of Asian-language dictionaries but now they're now second- and third-generation. Now we sell a lot of Portuguese and Eastern European dictionaries. I love the diversity of the area and it should be celebrated.'

Although she'll miss the statue of Moore, Hurst and Peters that lies across the Barking Road. 'It's a shame they're moving the statue. It's the last link, because they achieved it all here.'

Hopefully a lot of fans will still combine a trip to the Olympic Stadium with a visit to the Newham Bookshop, because Vivian feels her independent bookshop can offer more than the shops at Westfield. 'Stratford is full of chain stores, but the independents really know the area, so we really hope the fans do come and see us again next season.'

It's yet another facet of match day that I'll miss at Upton Park; but perhaps we all need to remember that the area will still be worth visiting after West Ham have gone. Never mind the gigantic Foyles at Westfield. Like many aficionados, I'll still be taking a detour to the Newham Bookshop to stock up on my literary bookings.

13

DRAWING DRAWING WEST HAM

A MOMENT OF MINOR STARDOM ARRIVES BEFORE THE FA Cup match at Manchester United; BT Sport film me in Ken's Café. It's for a feature on West Ham's FA Cup run and leaving the Boleyn.

We meet at 10 a.m. on a Tuesday morning in an unusually deserted Ken's Café. The three TV people spend a lot of time filming me buying a cup of tea from Carol and then walking through the door of Ken's – so perhaps it will end up with the action-thriller look. Producer Leah takes a big risk when she asks Carol to turn down the TV. Carol's doing her knitting and watching *MasterChef* and announces that this time is sacrosanct. Eventually she agrees to turn it down a notch and we do the interview with the TV on in the background, though Carol declines an interview with the BT crew herself.

We discuss the special atmosphere of the Boleyn and how hardened dockers wanted some footballing escapism. After the interview has finished, the cameraman asks for some slow-motion shots of me putting my West Ham hat on outside Ken's. I feel a bit like the Bruce Willis of E13.

The slot goes out on Thursday. It's an impressive piece and I'm quoted alongside Aaron Cresswell and Keith and Steve, two Hammers fans the TV crew has come across in the park. Cresswell talks about the unforgettable atmosphere at his first home game against Spurs and what a good manager Slaven is, while there's also plenty of slow-motion footage of Payet scoring against Blackburn. It has the obligatory shots of the John Lyall gates and the main stand and a soundtrack of the fans singing 'Bubbles'. Inside Ken's Café, there's myself saying it would mean everything to get to another Cup Final, though thankfully I don't make any firm predictions. Matt texts to say: 'One articulate young West Ham legend – and the other bloke is Pete May.'

The tickets for the Man United game have sold out in an hour on the phone, so having failed to get through in time I manage to beg a spare from Big Joe, who's in with the prawn sandwich-eaters, and dash over to his office in Clerkenwell to collect it.

'We've got Payet!' echoes around Euston station on Sunday morning as I make my way onto an utterly packed 11.20 a.m. train to Manchester. My return ticket has cost £82, but it seems like all 9,000 West Ham fans are on this particular train, which means standing for the whole journey. Next to me are two computer geeks, a Frenchman and American, who don't really like football but have been offered free corporate tickets by the Mancs and ask me what time the game kicks off.

From Manchester Piccadilly it's onto the X50 bus to Old Trafford. Tradition hangs heavy here, with a road called Sir Alex Ferguson Way and statues of Sir Matt Busby and Law, Best and Charlton. Outside the Bishop Blaize pub there's a flag that reads 'Chelmsford Reds' – presumably some of United's more local fans. Inside the stadium, the 9,000 West Ham fans are making a lot of noise and seem under the impression that that we have acquired a Reunion midfielder. I'm in with Big Joe's mate John and his son and the atmosphere is hugely expectant as we watch Payet practising free kicks in the pre-match warm-up.

West Ham start the game really confidently, with the excellent Noble again looking worthy of an England call-up. Andy Carroll plays Emenike through and the striker hits it wide when he should score. Cresswell crosses for Carroll to head powerfully over from a long way out and then another excellent move involving Noble, Payet and Cresswell sees Emenike head Aaron's cross into de Gea's arms. Andy Carroll would surely have buried that one. United look stodgy going forward, and their best effort sees Herrera balloon over when well placed.

West Ham continue to play well in the second half as Reid makes a great block, with United claiming handball (it bounced off his thigh onto his elbow). Payet pokes the ball past the immobile Fellaini and goes down in the box under a challenge from Rojo. In real time it looks a clear penalty, though replays later show that Payet appeared to go down very easily as his trailing foot was caught by Rojo. It's arguable either way, but still looks like simulation to my eyes, and Dmitri's surely better than that. It could have been a second yellow, too, for Payet had been booked in the first half.

The West Ham fans amuse themselves with chants of, 'Carlos Tevez – he left 'cos you're shit!'

On sixty-eight minutes, Payet wins a free-kick some thirty yards from United's goal. Surely he can't score from here? Dimitri pings in a sumptuous free kick that goes up and over the wall and dips into the net off the post as de Gea is left floundering. There's a second of stunned silence and then mayhem. Dimi runs to the far corner and kneels before the hushed United crowd. It's a sensational goal. On this form Payet could probably defeat Donald Trump, bring peace to

Syria and settle the EU referendum. Cue a mass of back-slapping and we've got Payeting in the away corner.

It looks like it could be a victory to rank with the Di Canio game of 1998, though United improve when they bring on Schweinsteiger. Bilić still goes for the second, bravely bringing on Sakho and Valencia.

It's never easy at Old Trafford, though. With seven minutes to go, Herrera crosses from the right and Martial arrives at the far post to poke home from a narrow angle. Old Trafford erupts with relief. The replays later show that Schweinsteiger has barged Randolph into the net as he goes for the cross and the goal should not have stood.

Commendably, West Ham still think they can win it at the end, gaining a series of corners. The willing Antonio takes the ball from the corner flag and thrillingly dribbles into the box before sending in a low shot that de Gea pushes wide at full-stretch. Great effort.

'Is there a fire drill?' chant the Irons fans at the Mancs heading for the exits.

The whistle blows and, although it's a chance lost, it's one final FA Cup game at Upton Park. And it's nice for a small club like United to get the money from a replay, though United's Europa League commitments mean it's many aeons away. Watford, Palace and Everton await the winners in the semi-finals. Could it finally be our year?

What's been really encouraging is the way the Hammers looked so confident and took the game to the home side. Admittedly Manchester United are looking stolid compared to the Fergie years, but it's still an intimidating place to come to. We looked like we believed we belonged in such an arena and, after wins at Arsenal, Liverpool and Manchester City and two draws at Man United, we are entitled to believe. You get the sense that West Ham are developing into a really good, mentally strong side.

'We'll race you back to London!' chant the West Ham crowd as the United fans leave in their Chevrolet-sponsored red shirts. The same chant is heard at the tram station, along with 'My name is Luděk Mikloško…' and, 'Oh, Christian Dailly, you are the love of my life!'

There's time for a pint of Pendle Witches Brew in the Piccadilly pub and some food in Go Falafel (falafel in Manchester?) before arriving at Piccadilly station, where there's a huge crush. With too many fans for the trains, the police kettle us behind the glass doors onto the platform. The crowd is kept behind barriers in a winding line and as the crush grows heavier, threatening to knock people over, it becomes positively scary. We're kept there for an hour and, rather than let people with reservations onto their trains, the police let people through on a first-come, first-served basis. I'm there at 7.20 p.m. for the 7.35 p.m. train, but no one is let through at all.

Despite chants of 'Hillsborough!' and 'You don't know what you're doing!', the Transport Police didn't make any announcements and nothing comes over the PA, so the passengers waiting get angrier and angrier. Red-faced policemen with crew cuts shout at us to move back. The crush gets worse. Eventually a barrier is kicked over and there's a rush for the doors when the police try to let people through in single file. There's a lot of pushing and shoving and one woman says she was accidentally hit when a policeman aimed a punch at a man who ducked. I eventually make it on to the 8.21 p.m. train and amazingly find a seat. At least the *Manchester Evening News* and the *Daily Mail* report the fiasco at the station the next day.

It's terrible policing, though not all the West Ham fans behave well on the way home either. I'm reminded of my first-ever glimpse of West Ham on a Cup run in 1975; deprived of success, when it does appear for a fleeting season, a few fans take it as a signal to outdrink George Best. The transport police on the train have to prevent several recidivists from stealing beer from the closed bar after its shutter is prized open. The police then seem to favour a quiet life when a group of drunken Herberts from Hornchurch sing anti-Semitic songs about Spurs for the final part of the journey.

But the problems of Sunday travel and boorish behaviour of some fans shouldn't diminish a wonderful goal and a great performance. Though, worryingly, Louis van Gaal's side have a habit of getting results in big games just when he's on the point of getting sacked.

Six days later, the Irons play at Stamford Bridge. We've failed to get tickets through the priority points system, but it sounds like a great game. It's a fantastic strike from distance by Lanzini for the opener, and there's not much anyone can do about Fabregas's free-kick equaliser (though the ref had the wall twelve yards back instead of ten). At 1-1, Cresswell shoots wide after a great move and back-heel from Lanzini, and then hits the bar. Big Andy Carroll comes on to poke home from Payet's pass and it looks like another glorious away day. Carroll has a header cleared off the line, but Chelsea's late equaliser comes from a disputed penalty. Antonio appears to have committed the offence outside the area, but the ref awards a penalty and Fabregas converts to make it 2-2.

Two seasons ago, West Ham were delighted to get a backs-to-the-wall 0-0 at Chelsea, now we're disappointed not to win. But the game is a credit to the Premier League – it's always good to see a small team like Chelsea with nothing to play for raise their game against Champions League contenders.

It's getting difficult, this business of being near the top of the league. Should we be grateful at getting a point at Chelsea or fuming because an incorrect penalty decision cost us two points and kept West Ham out of the top four? Should we be grateful to get a draw at Man United in the FA Cup or fuming that the ref missed Schweinsteiger's push on Randolph, this contributing to our fixture congestion and affecting our Champions League bid? Should we be targeting the Cup, the Champions League or the Europa League? And is it safe to say 'we're too good to go down' yet?

A two-week international hiatus follows, spliced with more good news for West Ham. Firstly, it's announced that the capacity at the Olympic Stadium is being increased from 54,000 to 60,000, and then that West Ham have signed the previously on-loan Manuel Lanzini for a reported £9 million. This in a season when Manchester United have spent £25 million on the underwhelming Memphis Depay, Man City squandered £42 million on defender Eliaquim Mangala and Liverpool spent £28 million on Christian Benteke (who doesn't appear to be rated by boss Jürgen Klopp).

Meanwhile, there's another stunning 37-yard free kick from Dimitri Payet for France against Russia. The French commentator is left drooling that it is 'exceptionelle!'

In the middle of a tense season, there's the pleasing interlude of Mark Noble's testimonial on the Easter Bank Holiday Monday. Despite the best efforts of TfL closing Upton Park Tube for planned maintenance – is this a tribute to the 2009/10 season, when we had to trek from Stratford, Canning Town and West Ham to watch the Hammers lose? – 35,000 fans make it to the Boleyn and are rewarded with West Ham beating West Ham All-Stars 6-5.

First it's a long walk from West Ham station and then a swift trip to Ken's Café where Michael, Matt and Lisa are in attendance. There's a great atmosphere in the ground and a bewildering array of old faces. Craig Bellamy still looks fit and scores the opener for the All-Stars. 'Come on, we can't lose to a team like West Ham!' I quip. Mark Noble gets the first for West Ham and Adrián runs the length of the field to bag one as well.

Anton and Rio Ferdinand play together in defence for the All-Stars; Dean Ashton is a few stones above his playing weight but scores a cracking overhead kick; Paolo Di Canio still has a great touch and feigns a bad back in one melodramatic touchline run; Carlton Cole still suffers from dodgy control; an early cameo from Dicksy gets a lot of cheers and Trevor Sinclair needs some extra-large shorts for his presenter's posterior. 'Oh, Christian Dailly, you are the love of my life!' greets the legendary football genius and he still looks match-fit, too, as he strolls through the game like a latter-day Beckenbauer.

Twelve-year-old Freddie Sears has a lot of energy from his Easter Eggs suggests Lisa, while a bulkier Marlon Harewood celebrates a goal (subsequently disallowed) by reprising his shirt-off FA Cup semi-final celebration. John Moncur makes some typically late tackles. We also get to see the return of Jimmy Walker, though sadly no return of his Walker's World column in the programme, where Lisa predicts he would be writing about 'Alex Song having himself with his dodgy gear'. Luděk Mikloško comes on to the obligatory song from the Bobby Moore Stand and keeps a clean sheet. Another highlight is Diafra Sakho groping down his shorts to find a phone and take a selfie after scoring. So the game may not be entirely serious.

It all ends in a penalty shoot-out, which West Ham both win and lose. Adrián manages to shoot over the bar but still slides on his knees to celebrate as he once did against Everton in the FA Cup.

Our walk to West Ham Tube afterwards is mitigated by a stop at the Black Lion, where the Old Bob is particularly fine and Michael confesses that he's planning on dyeing his hair claret and blue for the final home match at the Boleyn.

It's not often you get to see a stress-free West Ham game – even Matt hasn't got too cross with the ref – and a lot of money has been raised for three charities. A great day for Nobes, who's been a magnificent Hammer; there can't be many other players who would get 35,000 on a Tubeless Monday.

⚽ ⚽ ⚽

After a long fortnight, competitive football kicks off again with a Saturday match against Crystal Palace. In Ken's Café, Michael the Possible Whovian has brought along a bona fide Whovian in his Rangers-supporting mate Charlie, a man who has acted in Big Finish *Doctor Who* audio dramas and was once an auctioneer at a West Ham function (even if they had mistaken him for Charlie Ross off *Bargain Hunt*). We're joined by Lisa, a late replacement for Matt, who's suffering from lack of sleep and vertigo, and Nigel, who's just got a new job, narrowly avoiding becoming a DVD seller in the Central. There's a late cameo from DC and his wee man and, astonishingly, Michael gets to eat his big breakfast before the kick-off.

'We're playing a team that hasn't won in 2016. What could possibly go wrong?' I venture at the kick-off.

It's lucky Matt is absent, as you'd fear for his karma with Mark Clattenburg in charge. Early on, Clattenburg waves play on after Emenike is felled on the edge of the box, setting the tone for an erratic performance. Soon he's booked Noble and Reid.

Palace's luck appears to have changed after fifteen minutes, as Adrián palms a free kick up in the air and straight on to the head of Delaney, who heads home from a tight angle. It's a rare error from a keeper who's had a great season.

But Palace betray their lack of confidence by conceding within three minutes. Antonio overlaps to get in a fine cross, Sakho heads it back and it's deflected by a defender into the path of Manuel Lanzini, who controls in an instant and fires past Hennessey. That's Manuel's seventh of the season.

Palace isn't the easy match many anticipated, though, and at 1-1 Puncheon knees over an inviting cross from Bolasie.

But the thing is, we've got Payet. Dimitri has already sent one early free kick over the bar when he's felled by Ward on the edge of the box. This time Hennessey puts seven defenders in the wall, but it might as well be seventeen, as Payet simply pings the ball up into the stratosphere and then dipping into the top corner. A sumptuous goal and the whole ground bursts into a rapturous 'We've got Payet!' It's still sung in a tone of incredulity by most fans. We've got the East End Messi. Chief Engineer Montgomery Scott has just been proved wrong; you can change the laws of physics, Captain.

Nigel's happy that 'Welcome to the Jungle' by Guns N' Roses comes on the PA at half-time and all seems for the best in the best of all possible worlds as we then spot Time Lord Donald Sumpter in the concourse. Michael and Charlie ponder whether to say 'Get off my planet!' to him as we consider appearing at the final home game in full Time Lord regalia.

It's a scrappy start to the second half, though, and West Ham are not looking like a Champions League side. Kouyaté plays a poor back pass, forcing Adrián to dash from his goal and make a desperate save. The ball falls to Sako and only a brilliant goal line clearance by Cresswell prevents a goal.

With his mind still on that dodgy back pass, Kouyaté miscontrols and lunges into a sliding tackle on Gayle. He wins the ball but his feet are off the ground and Clattenburg gives a straight red. Harsh, as a yellow would surely have been sufficient since it was a clumsy rather than malicious challenge. Though Kouyaté, who's been a powerful presence all season, should have known not to take chances with a ref like Clattenburg, who probably goes to sleep counting yellow cards.

'It's always difficult to play against ten men,' I counsel, though Palace don't seem to agree. Our subs don't work either, as Valencia still looks jet-lagged after international duty and Carroll doesn't get much service and mainly fires shots into defenders' legs.

'You're just a c**t with a whistle!' chant the home fans.

'Good old East End wit,' muses Nigel.

There's a warning when Sako volleys horribly wide from Bolasie's cross. Palace equalise with a bit of a comedy goal as Ogbonna volleys Souaré's cross against the legs of Reid and Dwight Gayle pounces for an easy finish and celebrates in front of the away fans.

The stadium clocks have still stopped, and as time seems to coagulate it's a case of respect the point at this stage, as only a great block from Reid denies Sako a winner. The final whistle blows to a rousing chorus of 'The referee's a wanker!'

Still, maybe it's a sign of progress that a draw feels like a defeat. Man City have won 4-0, so fourth seems a long way off again. We retreat to the Central where the dodgy DVD seller is back, the Old Speckled Hen is chilled and Michael and Charlie are looking forward to an evening watching 'East End Edna' at the Carpenters in King's Cross.

A shame Payet's goal didn't win it as we've seen another moment of genius. But as Slaven says, we have to keep playing football and get on with it. Perhaps the pressure got to West Ham a little today, and we need to cut out the defensive errors in the six-pointer against Arsenal. We can't blame it all on the ref as both goals came from defensive errors and the side had stuttered even before Kouyaté was sent off.

By the following Tuesday, Kouyaté's red card has been rescinded, proving that West Ham are more rescinded against than sinning. It's the third red card West Ham have had overturned this season: the others being Mark Noble against Liverpool and Kouyaté against Blackburn. It won't bring back the two points West Ham dropped, but the good news is Kouyaté's available to face Arsenal.

It's another TV-dictated early kick-off of 12.45 p.m. on Saturday for the Gunners match. If budget airlines can fly at two in the morning, you expect the TV companies will soon be scheduling games for then. In Ken's Café, Michael and Matt are discussing Mark Almond musicals as we wonder if Nigel thinks it's a 3 p.m. kick-off. He makes a very late appearance to confirm that he hates Soft Cell even more than the Smiths. There's a long wait at high noon as we make a late bid to get served and this time it's me who has to demolish egg, chips and beans in two minutes at 12.35 p.m.

We make a late run to the East Stand, where writing student Fraser is mentally composing his Victorian novel about gunslingers that isn't a Western. Diafra Sakho is missing from the squad having reported a knee injury on the eve of the match.

Even at 12.45 p.m. there's a great atmosphere in the stadium and a rousing 'We've got Payet!' going round all four stands. Andy Carroll picks up a needless booking in the third minute by fouling Koscielny and we all worry that he's too fired up. A few minutes later, Carroll's overhead kick is headed into the net by Lanzini but is incorrectly disallowed for off-side by referee Craig Pawson. That's four games in a row where the Hammers have suffered from debatable decisions. Infamy, infamy…

So, almost a great start, but Slaven's back-five formation, with Tomkins and Antonio on the right, is looking unsure, and Reid and Ogbonna are having trouble tracking the runs of Sánchez. Monreal dives in the box and is still on the ground claiming a penalty as Iwobi finds Özil. The prone and offside Monreal moves out of Özil's way to allow the Gunner to score as West Ham vainly appeal for offside.

'You're just a c**t with a whistle!' goes up from the home fans.

It gets worse after thirty-five minutes as Iwobi finds Sánchez, who has drifted through our defence and slots home.

'You're gonna win f**k all!' sing the gleeful Arsenal fans.

'We could be on for a heavy beating here,' suggests Nigel.

'Could be another 4-0,' I concur.

Antonio rouses the crowd by winning a tackle and playing a fine crossfield ball and Carroll turns and has a decent shot saved. But we're still looking to keep it down to 2-0 and regroup at half-time.

'Arsenal are like Leicester but with a Rolls-Royce defence,' muses Michael, as I suggest, rather hopefully, that the Gunners might still be suspect at the back.

On forty-four minutes comes some hope. Cresswell swings in a cross and Carroll is allowed time to get a run on Gabriel and head home. That will change things before half-time. Only it gets better. In added time, a West Ham corner is punched clear by Ospina and Noble does really well to beat his man and cross it back in. Andy Carroll mis-hits his first shot against Gabriel, but then athletically volleys home the rebound to cause pandemonium at the Boleyn. He runs towards the corner of the Betway and Trevor Brooking stands doing his arms-outstretched, Angel of the North celebration. Two-all and what a half.

Matt notes that the PA is playing the Cult at half-time and we wonder if the referee is indeed a cult with a whistle. Instead of discussing how to keep the score down, we're now talking about whether Andy Carroll could get a hat-trick and go to the Euros with England. Though he's also the sort of player who might then get sent off for taking off his shirt while celebrating.

Emenike comes on for Tomkins as West Ham revert to a flat back four and start the second half by continuing to attack the Gunners. Arsenal complain as Carroll escapes censure for jumping with an arm in Gabriel's face, but it looks accidental – Carroll is looking at the ball when jumping.

Lanzini has a penalty appeal turned down. Carroll chases down Koscielny in the fashion of an escaped bullock, causing the Arsenal defender to get in a hopeless muddle with Ospina. Payet taps the loose ball home. It looks like a 50/50 tussle, but ref Pawson disallows another West Ham goal.

West Ham will not be thwarted; Andy Carroll plays a great ball out wide to Antonio on the right. The Shakespearian winger beats Monreal and dinks in a great cross for Carroll to hang above Bellerín and power home a header for a seven-minute hat-trick. Cue an eruption of arms in the Bobby Moore Stand as Andy runs over to our corner flag and Mark Noble sensibly jumps on him to ensure he keeps his shirt on. It has to be Carroll's best performance for the Hammers.

'Who are yer! Who are yer!' and 'Two-nil and you f**ked it up!' chant the WHU fans.

To their credit, Arsenal keep calm and come back into the game, with Özil prominent. Lanzini clears off the line from Monreal and Arsenal bring on Giroud and Ramsey, which is worrying. The Gooners equalise when Giroud's clever flick to Özil sees Welbeck mishit the ball to Koscielny, who fires home. Winston Reid should probably have been a bit tighter.

There's still time for Ospina to nervously tip away efforts from Payet and Cresswell as both sides go for the winner. Payet makes a great run in from the left, but chooses the wrong option after beating three players.

The tension's getting to Matt, who in language the Archbishop of Canterbury might not approve of, berates Adrián for making a poor clearance, Dimitri for not passing to Emenike ('What's the point of that? He's waiting for a free kick that this ref's never going to give!') and Craig Pawson for not sending off Gabriel for kicking out at Carroll – the Arsenal man escapes as the ref has already penalised Big Andy for a foul.

It's breathless stuff and like one of the mad, high-scoring games from the Ron Greenwood era. Well, we wanted to be entertained, and nobody respects the point here. Somehow it ends at 3-3 and 'Bubbles' and 'If the Kids Are United' comes on the PA as the players salute the crowd. It's four games in a row now that West Ham have suffered from dubious decisions and we wonder if there's a conspiracy against us organised by the CIA, aliens from Roswell and whoever blew up the third tower at 9/11 and faked the moon landings.

So it's off to the beer garden at the Central, where we muse over a fantastic game among the iffy charity collectors and DVD sellers as we wait for Matt's mate Peggsy. A point won't get us into the Champions League and some dodgy refereeing has cost us again – but after a game like that, who really cares?

14

WIN OR LOSE WE'RE ON THE BOOZE

FOR THE PUBS AROUND WEST HAM, IT'S CLOSING TIME... For many, the loss of the football club will prove terminal. Everyone has their pre- and post-match rituals and otherwise underwhelming pubs have been kept going by the match-day influx.

All sorts of idiosyncratic boozers have come and gone. Behind the lengthy queue for Upton Park Tube station there was a strange pub in what appeared to be a suburban house; the lonely sign for the Prince of Wales still stands in Prince's Terrace, though the pub itself has reverted to housing.

My fellow season-ticket holder Fraser remembers: 'The police would patrol it every twenty minutes on match days, which oddly enough didn't make it feel any safer. I used to pop in before a game to meet my friend Keith. Once he told me he'd heard someone point at us while we were each carrying a *Guardian* and say accusingly, "Look at those bastards, they can read."'

'The Prince made the Central look like Harry's Bar in Venice,' recalls my pal Matt. 'Some random bloke would jump on the pool table and sing Hammers songs very badly. Fraser once bought a CD of his "singing" from him. I don't think he felt he had a choice.'

In recent years my party has favoured the Central in Barking Road, mainly because of its ease of access for getting a late Tube home after evening games. It's a spacious old pub with a large front bar and a back bar where satellite football plays on a giant screen and a disused stage stands in the corner. Big Joe has never forgotten the posters offering weekly entertainment from Two Bob Ray and Smooth Steve.

Other forms of entertainment tend to be self-made. After an evening game against Spurs, noting an empty table in the front bar by the window, Michael and Fraser attempted to take a seat. An indignant young lady told them it was her table. She needed to be there, she said, so she could flash at the Spurs fans' coach parked outside – which she proceeded to do.

After every game a woman selling a bag of dodgily recorded DVDs of the latest films glides through the drinkers like Martin Peters ghosting in at the far post. She's at least ten minutes ahead of drinking-up time. Wonder if she'll be turning up in Stratford next season trying to sell the latest blockbusters (complete with audience coughs) to John Lewis?

Malcolm Allison was once spotted sitting in the front bar one afternoon drinking a glass of their finest red wine – possibly the only man ever to drink wine in the confines of the Central.

It can often take an age to get served and the beer is not exactly craft. For some years a solitary hand pump offered hope, though it never actually had any bitter flowing along its pipes. A gassy version of cold IPA did appear – but not with a hand pump – and then in recent years bottles of Old Speckled Hen have offered some salvation for the discerning drinker, though the staff often think it should be chilled (apologising if it isn't) and others think it's a cider.

At the back of the pub is a large but sparse garden with some tables on grass and in one corner what appears to be a mix of demolished outhouses where promised extra rooms never quite materialise. It was in the garden that we once met an extremely drunk pair of Norwegian fans. Despite looking like bearded Hell's Angels, it later emerged that one of them was in the police force and the other was a taxi driver, both having cultivated an unlikely Scandinavian allegiance to the Irons. Their lager consumption suggested it would not be a good plan to either take a taxi or get arrested in Norway.

The Central now offers rooms for backpackers and ushers out drinkers early – often by the unsubtle act of turning up the techno to eleven – so they can prepare the breakfast tables. After a few pints we often imagine travellers asking for a room in central London, only to find themselves in the Central, forlornly looking for Oxford Street outside.

The first pub I ever went into at West Ham was the Queen's by Queen's Market. It's the closest pub to Upton Park Tube and those early 1970s memories involve interminable waits among side-burned blokes in Oxford Bags before getting served with cold keg beer in plastic skiffs. These days, bouncers in bomber jackets stand guard on match days. It's a low-ceilinged modern boozer with pictures of Frank McAvennie, Billy Bonds, Alvin Martin, Bobby Moore and the 1964 FA Cup-winning side adorning the walls. The one advantage of the Queen's, though, is that the loo is straight down the stairs to the right of the entrance – when desperate to relieve yourself it's easy to use the gents without actually buying any beer.

It was also pretty weird seeing the Queen's on the national news while holidaying in Yorkshire in 2009. Sitting in a borrowed house in Shipley, scenes of mayhem appeared on our TV screens as Millwall and West Ham fans fought battles with each other and the police. The Queen's looked like it was in downtown Rome as the Barbarians, Visigoths and Vandals charged.

The most famous Hammers pub close to the stadium is the Boleyn, complete with its 'no away supporters' sign. It's an imposing old Victorian pub that is a Grade II-listed building. It's also on CAMRA's (Campaign for Real Ale) Inventory of Historic Pub Interiors. Look at it on a non-match day and you'll observe lots of fine wood features and stained glass. At one end of the pub stands the former billiards room with a beautiful stained-glass skylight and moulded frieze. It's here that you'll encounter the stickiest pub carpet in London on match days. DMs are instantly attached to the soggy fibres and it can feel a little like walking on the surface of a very high-gravity, beery planet.

The Boleyn has, reputedly, the longest horseshoe bar in London. To the right of the Green Street door stands a small wooden snug bar where the hardiest locals congregate. There are two other larger bars and also a small open yard that takes you right back to the days of dockers and sugar refinery workers, with wooden doors that open out onto Green Street for easy horse-and-cart access.

On match days, the main areas are a heaving mass of West Ham fans. 'Bubbles' is played at full volume as beer flies through the air and everyone has a sing-song. The music is always loud and it's a Bacchanalian maelstrom compared to the Central. We did once find London Pride on sale in the back bar, though it wasn't particularly well kept, but mainly it's a lager-and-Guinness type of boozer.

Look at any of the old pictures of the West Ham players celebrating the FA Cup wins of 1964, 1975 and 1980, and the coach is invariably in front of the Boleyn. After West Ham's 1980 FA Cup win, I ended up at the Boleyn with my Brentwood mates. Beer had been imbibed and at one point a group of lads ceremonially placed an Arsenal scarf on the floor and burnt it. Not sure if that would pass health-and-safety regulations today.

The Boleyn is offering fans a £120 per year membership scheme when West Ham move to the Olympic Stadium; for their money they'll be able to still drink in the Boleyn and take a free coach to the new ground. Hopefully this might save the grand old boozer. If the fine old Victorian interiors of the Boleyn were in Islington it would surely be gentrified and turned into a gastro pub.

Many fans have opted for pubs further away from the stadium to solve the perennial problem of trying to get bar service.

My mate Gavin spent two and a half years living near the ground in the late 1980s: 'I remember being given a big hug by the retired François Van der Elst in the Miller's Well at

East Ham. I'd heard François was a beer lover, and that he'd be there that day. No sooner had I said that it was good to meet him, and I was hugged like an old relative.'

Gavin adopted the Upton Manor Tavern in Plashet Road as his local. He recalls a *Minder*-esque array of characters, including a man claiming to be Jermain Defoe's dad who'd ask for drinks, a customer just out of prison who insisted he lent him a tenner (and got rather threatening when asked for its return) and a muscular black geezer known as 'The Mediator' or 'Acas', who always seemed to be breaking up arguments around the pool table. 'He was someone to approach with caution if he wasn't mediating,' recalls Gavin. 'I once saw him with a knife, and another time with one of those wobbly things you used to hang on to if you were standing up on the Tube. He threatened one of the builders with a knife outside the pub. The builder was eventually allowed to go, and said to me in the pub later: "If you just act calm you'll be OK. If I'd got all excited, he probably would have knifed me."'

'The Upton Manor played Irish country music, and people occasionally got up to dance, especially at weekends, when there were always lock-ins,' continues Gavin. 'I enjoyed going to the Manor for a few pints before West Ham games. There were a couple of times when I was enjoying it so much that I didn't bother turning up to the match.

'I remember watching the Spurs versus Coventry FA Cup

Final there in 1987 when somebody told me Guinness was good if you drunk it through a straw. After many pints, the aftermath of the game became a complete blur and I later ended up asleep on the platform at Hammersmith station. Someone had nicked my glasses.'

Arriving at the pub after a match in the late 1980s, Gavin and Fraser discovered that the Manor was now employing strippers. Fraser takes up the story: 'We repaired to the garden instead, only to be followed by an angry stripper demanding we pay her anyway. Gavin refused on the grounds that he wouldn't be able to see her from the garden. There was a moment where she seemed to consider performing her act al fresco just to wheedle some money from us. Mercifully she changed her mind after we gave her a few coins.'

My favourite pub, as a Real Ale drinker, has always been the Black Lion at Plaistow. It's a fair walk from the ground, but always worth it for the Maldon Gold, Old Bob and Adnams ale on sale in the cosy back bar. It's one of the oldest buildings in Plaistow. The front is Victorian, but go through the arch and you're in a proper old coach yard with stables and outbuildings. The pub is said to date from at least 1742, and might even have links with not-so-dandy highwayman Dick Turpin, who ran a smuggling racket between Plaistow and Southend and started his nefarious activities by nicking a couple of oxen from a local Plaistow farmer.

Something of the spirit of Dick Turpin lives on. Fraser was once waiting hours for one of us to get served and struck up a conversation with a man in the garden who asked if he'd been going to West Ham for long.

'My dad used to bring me as a kid,' answered Fraser.

'I used to bring my son when he was young,' the garden drinker replied wistfully.

'Does he not bother now he's grown up?' enquired Fraser.

'He can't. He's in prison.'

The Black Lion also has a proper historic link with West Ham, as the players, including Booby Moore, Geoff Hurst, Frank Lampard and briefly Jimmy Greaves, used to drink there in the glory days of the 1970s. According to Harry Redknapp: 'Me, Bobby Moore and our mates used to get into the Black Lion pub round the corner to the ground at half-five after the match, have a drink and nobody bothered us.'

At the back of the pub two claret-and-blue-painted walls reveal where the famous West Ham Amateur Boxing Club once trained. There's another bar at the back and a large garden, which is packed in summer. It feels warm and welcoming and surely has a post-football future.

The ghosts of other pubs haunt the streets. Turn left at the Tube down Green Street and you'll find some closed shutters and the remnants of the sign for the Duke of Edinburgh.

The Duke was the most popular pub for away fans and was always rammed on match day.

At the crossroads of Barking Road and Greengate Road stood the Castle. It was painted claret and blue and we ended up there in the snow – all the other pubs had shut early – after West Ham had beaten Man United 4-0 in the League Cup in 2010 and Jonathan Spector had improbably scored twice. The Castle has now shut its doors for ever and has unceremoniously become a branch of Betfred. Opposite the Castle was the Greengate, which was often mysteriously short of beer, even on match days, and is now a Tesco Express.

Over the years, fans have developed an allegiance to many other pubs, some still open, some not, such as the Earl of Wakefield, the Denmark Arms, the Lord Stanley, the Green Man, the Victoria Tavern and even boxer Terry Marsh's bar on Green Street, full of boxing memorabilia.

But now the pub apocalypse is here. Most of the Muslim community in Newham don't drink alcohol – which is no bad thing in terms of the ills it can cause – and the area has, like the rest of Britain, moved more towards home drinking, restaurants, coffee bars and cafés. But a piece of local history goes every time one of the old boozers closes. Hopefully the influx of affluent flat-owners on the site of the Boleyn Ground will help keep at least a few of them open.

Will we ever find the equivalent boozers in Stratford,

complete with sticky carpets, bad beer, dodgy DVD sellers, geezers out of prison, blokes singing on top of pool tables, women flashing at the Spurs coach and François Van der Elst, Big Mal and Mooro at the bar?

Probably not, though there is a nice craft beer place with designer pizzas and hipster beards by Hackney Wick ... and perhaps someone will do a pop-up Prince of Wales, complete with a bloke singing on the pool table and regular visits from the Old Bill.

15

CONCENTRATING ON THE EUROPA LEAGUE

WILL THE FA CUP REPLAY AGAINST MAN UNITED BE THE defining game of our season? It's a little worrying that the programme has pictures of our three FA Cup wins on the front cover and the *Evening Standard* has a double-page spread on 'One Last Knockout Night', with Cup memories from Peter Brabrook, Billy Bonds, Ray Stewart, Tony Gale and Aaron Cresswell. But it's never going to be an easy game against a Man United side fighting to save LVG's job.

Taking an early stroll up Green Street, there's a Pearly King, complete with a West Ham badge on his suit, buying a programme outside the John Lyall gates. Fans are stopping to take selfies with him.

Matt, Lisa and her pal Sue, Michael and myself are in Ken's Café ridiculously early thanks to the 7 p.m. kick-off – another time of maximum inconvenience on this occasion dictated by the BBC's FA Cup coverage. We're all feeling nervous and causing consternation to young Billy on waiting duties by pulling a fifth chair round our table. Even DC and his wee man arrive early, suggesting something's in the air at Upton Park.

We arrive in the East Stand unusually early too, beating Fraser for once. For years we thought he must be in the stand forty-five minutes before kick-off. But actually he's almost as tardy as us Ken's Café diners. Strangely, Michael is tempted by a plastic bottle of stadium Carlsberg as they're right out of craft beer.

There's a vibrant, beery atmosphere at the start of the match, but it's soon evident that the air of expectation might have affected West Ham. United look solid, with Rashford and Martial impressing up front and Fosu-Mensah looking a real prospect at the back. As usual, Fellaini, hated by the Manchester fans, looks really impressive against us.

'Where's your famous atmosphere?' chant the cheeky Mancs supporters.

'Live round the corner … You only live round the corner!' comes the response from the Bobby Moore Stand.

Rain pounds the Upton Park pitch and drifts evocatively

beneath the lights. Valencia puts a tame effort straight at de Gea early on, while Randolph makes fine saves from Fellaini's deflected shot and Lingard's low effort. It's goalless at half-time and Matt, who's sitting alone in Row D tonight, gives us a long tactical analysis of what's going wrong with Noble, Payet and Valencia. 'Geno' by Dexys comes on the PA, presumably as a tribute to Slaven Bilić's Kevin Rowland-style beanie hat.

We return to our seats. Nine minutes into the second half, inspiration arrives for Man United. Antonio's pass is blocked and Martial finds Rashford, who shows superb footwork to jink between Tomkins and Ogbonna and curl a brilliant effort into the top corner. Thirteen minutes later it's 2-0 as Lingard crosses and Martial's shot deflects off a defender onto Fellaini's thigh and into the net. Oh, sod it…

A rainbow appears above the East Stand, but there's no Cup of gold at the end of it for West Ham.

We play a lot better when the pressure's off. De Gea makes a fantastic save to deny Antonio's prod towards goal from Payet's corner. On seventy-nine minutes, West Ham pull a goal back. From another Payet corner Andy Carroll gets in a towering header and Tomkins bravely stoops to head home.

Suddenly there's hope we can eke out another thirty minutes of Cup football at Upton Park and there's a collective East End roar. Carroll flashes a header just over from

Cresswell's cross. In added time, Payet's cross is deflected into the path of Kouyaté and de Gea makes a great save. The ball rebounds to Carroll, who fires in another stinging shot only to be denied by the keeper again. Kouyaté heads home from de Gea's parry of Andy's shot, but is ruled marginally offside.

Our final corner sums up the evening as Payet finds Noble on the edge of the box only for Nobes to volley wildly wide. The Mancs keep the ball to a chorus of 'olés' from their fans as the whistle blows and they make the semi-final at Wembley.

We slump towards the Central. Perhaps the deflating of dreams is a more fitting historical tribute to the Boleyn Ground. At least we can't mess it up against Everton, Watford or Palace now. And Payet might be less in demand. Michael will be able to go to a day of events celebrating the 400th anniversary of Shakespeare's birth and Fraser will be able to pitch to a meeting of literary agents on 21 May. And I might be able to plan a mini-break in the Lake District. Take the positives. It's a devalued competition and big teams concentrate on getting into the Champions League.

The mood is thoroughly deflated in the pub. There's hardly anyone in there and now we know our name was never on the Cup, even in pencil.

'It's the first time we've felt like this since August,' says Fraser, which is a good point; we've had a fantastic home run since losing to Bournemouth, going sixteen games undefeated.

At least there's a big game coming up against league-leaders Leicester. After my third pint of Old Speckled Hen, Michael the Whovian offers advice on my moral dilemma: do we want to beat Leicester on Sunday and hand the title to Spurs or should we be wanting Leicester to win the league for the greater good of football? It would after all be one of the greatest achievements in sporting history and prove that money doesn't count for everything in the Premier League. I'm agonising like Tom Baker in 'Genesis of the Daleks', when he has the chance to destroy the Daleks at birth but asks, 'Do I have the right?'

'You, the chronicler of West Ham, should not be entertaining these thoughts... If the price of West Ham qualifying for the Champions League is Spurs winning the league, which is the greater good?' intones Michael like a latter-day Polonius to my Laertes. Though, knowing West Ham, we might win the league for Spurs and then fail to get into both the Europa League or the Champions League.

Fuddled by ale and despair and moral quandaries, I forget my bag and dash back from the Barking Road to retrieve it from the breakfast tables for the backpackers. My solitary walk to the station takes me past police dealing with an argument outside the Boleyn and the bouncers at the Queens having a row with some punters. Not the way we wanted to say farewell to cup nights at Upton Park.

There are six games left and we can still achieve something special. But, for now, our Cup Final breakfast at Nigel's house in Kew is going to have to be postponed for another season. Thirty-seven years of hurt never stopped me dreaming…

The next day I visit the Newham Bookshop to interview Vivian Archer, feeling tired and suffering from concentrating on the league ennui. Walking down a somnolent Green Street as street cleaners clear the detritus from last night. Ken's Café is shut. Where is it now, the vision and the gleam?

Since we last reached the FA Cup Final in 2006, Aston Villa, Hull City, Wigan, Stoke, Portsmouth, Everton and Cardiff have all reached finals. Since West Ham last reached the League Cup Final in 1981, it's been won by Swansea City, Birmingham City, Blackburn, Leicester, Aston Villa, Sheffield Wednesday, Nottingham Forest, Luton, Oxford and Norwich. We're bigger than most of those clubs. Surely West Ham's time must come?

On Sunday it's an 8.45 a.m. start on the Holloway Road as Nigel and I are picked up by Gavin and his neighbour David, an Arsenal fan turned football connoisseur who's driving to the match.

At least it's exciting to be witnessing Leicester's astonishing rise to the verge of the Premier League title – though I still have a suspicion Spurs will catch them. And, I tell myself, West Ham can still make the top five and even the Champions League spots.

Gavin is wearing his 'revolutionary hardwearing slippers' to the match, which are very comfortable, if not as intimidating as DMs should we meet any Leicester hoolies. Nigel has recovered from his cup ennui by seeing Stevenage versus Newport yesterday and informs us he's got a new Panini sticker album. On the same day, Gav was spotting hipsters at Dulwich Hamlet versus Lewes, which makes me feel like a very poor ground-hopper as I was walking the dog with my wife in Clissold Park.

We have a good journey in David's motor and arrive in Leicester two hours before kick-off. We park in Hazel Road, as Nigel points out the useful fact that all the local roads around the old Filbert Street area are named after nuts, and that Filbert is actually a type of nut too. Though Brazil Street wasn't named after Alan Brazil.

We manage to park for a fiver and then Nigel tries to take us into the Leicester Tigers rugby ground. After reorienting, we find the King Power Stadium and have a slap-up lunch of omelette, chips and beans at the café in the nearby Morrisons.

We walk to the stadium past stalls selling scarves reading 'Leicester: Fearless Champions' and remark that West Ham fans would never, ever tempt fate by such presumptuousness.

Inside the King Power, the home fans are busy chanting: 'We're Leicester City, we're top of the league!' as the West Ham corner responds with 'We've got Payet!'

Our seats are in row CC, which Nigel thinks is a good omen as it reminds him of Carlton Cole. After much fanfare on the PA and a guard of schoolchildren, the local heroes emerge and we kick off.

One minute into the game, West Ham win a free kick. Payet drops the ball onto Kouyaté's head and Schmeichel makes a fantastic save to tip the ball onto the post. It rolls along the line onto the other post and back into the keeper's arms. We're not getting any luck at all.

Huth goes close with a header but it's mainly West Ham attacking for the first fifteen minutes. But that's when Leicester are at their most dangerous. From a West Ham corner, Schmeichel's quick throw finds Mahrez on the right. He passes inside to Kanté and the midfielder plays a fine ball through to Vardy, who has outpaced Antonio and Ogbonna and takes one touch before slotting a crisp finish into the corner.

'That was lethal,' says Nigel.

'Jamie Vardy's having a party! Jamie Vardy's having a party!' chant the home fans.

It's 1-0 at half-time and Gavin points out no less a figure than Marlon Harewood wearing a blue hoodie in the away end. It's the best West Ham legend spot since we once saw Trevor Morley and Ian Bishop among the away fans at Arsenal.

With Huth and Morgan looking strong at the back, it looks like the usual 1-0 win for Leicester as the second half begins. Vardy just fails to connect with Okazaki's cross, but, with Carroll on for Obiang, West Ham are offering more attacking threat. The game changes on fifty-six minutes. Vardy tangles with Ogbonna in the West Ham box and goes down. Ref Jonathan Moss gives Vardy a second yellow card for simulation. He's already been booked for a foul in the first half and he's off. Replays show only mild contact with Ogbonna and Vardy throwing his legs towards Angelo. Looks like a dive to me and a correct decision.

'Jamie Vardy's having a shower! Jamie Vardy's having a shower!' chant the Hammers fans.

With Lanzini on for Noble, West Ham start to dominate against ten men. Winston Reid hits the outside of the post with a clever flick from Payet's cross. But Huth is heading everything that moves and it looks likes Leicester, with their incredible team spirit, will hold out.

West Ham win a corner with seven minutes left. Before it's taken, ref Moss gives Huth and Morgan a lecture on grappling in the box. Morgan then pulls back Winston Reid and the ref awards a spot-kick. Leicester fans throw their silly paper clappers onto the pitch in protest. Andy Carroll calmly dispatches the penalty to start his own party, running towards us in the away section.

It was a definite penalty, but just about every challenge from every corner should have been a penalty. There's been a tremendous amount of grappling in the box and referee Moss clearly gave the spot-kick because, even though such holding happens all the time, he had specifically warned Huth, Morgan and co. seconds before. West Ham could have been penalised at times too. In some ways it's been encouraging to watch Angelo Ogbonna match Huth in the dark arts of holding and tugging (he did learn his trade in Italy after all), as West Ham are clearly not going to be intimidated by Huth and Morgan's gamesmanship.

Slaven Bilić is an animated figure on the touchline, urging West Ham forward. He's not going to settle for a point and clearly doesn't buy into the Leicester fairy tale.

Two minutes later, Antonio does brilliantly to skip around two defenders and get in a cross. The ball is half-headed clear but Aaron Cresswell sends an unstoppable half-volley into the top of the net. What a goal. The West Ham fans go 'effing mental.

'1-0 and you f**ked it up!' chant the Irons fans, followed

by the not very witty but certainly concise 'You're f**king shit, you're f**king shit!'

Are we heading for a win at last? It seems so as ref Moss ignores a valid penalty appeal as Ogbonna holds down Huth in the box and the home crowd explodes with indignation.

We're into the fourth minute of added time as Nigel rages at Valencia for losing possession instead of hoofing the ball downfield. Schlupp is running into the edge of the box and tumbles after an innocuous challenge from Andy Carroll. Big Andy should have jockeyed him rather than tried to play the ball, but it was never a penalty and the ref appears to have been swayed by the ire of the crowd at his earlier decision to give West Ham a penalty. Claudio Ranieri stands, arms folded, in his technical area. Ulloa calmly slots home to send the Leicester fans into massive celebrations.

'2-1 and you f**ked it up!' chant the Leicester fans as the whistle blows, before both sets of drained supporters join in some anti-Tottenham chants.

A cracking game, even if it ended in the usual dodgy decision going against the Irons. The consolation is that at least we haven't won the title for Spurs and I've been proud of the way West Ham wanted to get something from this match after the disappointment of the Man United game.

We head off to the Counting House, which serves IPA and London Glory ales. A Leicester fan tells us they'd have settled for top half at the start of the season and has some interesting stories about Foxes legend Alan Birchenall. When he asks Gavin to name a Leicester full-back who played for England, he's astonished when Gavin gets Steve Whitworth – 'Brilliant! Steve Whitworth! Fooking Statto!'

We receive a number of texts from a tired and emotional Matt, who's been on the night shift. We can imagine his fingers angrily pounding the phone as he rages against Leicester, Valencia and former Culture Club drummer Jonathan Moss for being rubbish.

'No sugar-coating it, that was utterly unprofessional Noble, Payet etc. believing the hype, not a penalty re Carroll but he shouldn't have been there and given ref a decision to make. Emenike awful. Bilić needs to show he can be a good manager now as the season is falling apart. Against ten men you have to see the game out. You probably didn't spot Valencia aimlessly giving the ball away when we win if he keeps possession. But never a penalty and even Heskey and Lineker are admitting it. Have to say Leicester look a really mediocre team. They basically had one chance. Anyway I have to go to bed now,' reads Matt's incendiary text.

But we have got a point at the likely champions. The Leicester fans are still singing that they're top of the league. The West Ham fans' chant of 'Leicester's a shithole, I wanna go home!' is answered with 'F**k off to your tower blocks!', sung to the tune of 'Go West'. We retreat to David's VW Golf and head back down the M1, having to endure a very long wait for a coffee at the services and listening to lots of angry Hammers fans phoning Ian Wright and Kelly Cates complaining about poor decisions against Man United, Chelsea, Palace, Arsenal and Leicester. Some conspiracy theorists are even suggesting that UEFA didn't want another 'small team' in the Champions League alongside Leicester.

Four games left now and we've drawn four – admittedly very entertaining – league games in a row, we reflect as we f**k off back to our tower blocks. Champions League looks difficult now.

West Ham's fourth game in a fortnight arrives with the visit of Watford to Upton Park. Michael the Whovian has pre-ordered his big breakfast through Lisa as we join the Ken's Café queue. Nigel's running late at the office and Matt is working. Statto Lisa reveals that Andy Carroll's penalty at Leicester was our first away penalty for five years. Meanwhile, Carol's grandson Billy is very impressed with seeing Ken's Café on BT Sport.

After the food arrives, Carol leaves her till and sits down next to Michael, declaring affectionately, 'You really love your big breakfasts, don't you?' Michael says he doesn't have them at home (where it's presumably only Ottolenghi salads), which is why they're such a treat.

In the East Stand, we are joined by Fraser, the Raymond Chandler of the East Stand, who has just won second prize in a short-story competition, but has forgotten his laptop, so he can't turn out today's 2,300 words in the Central.

It's good to see Diafra Sakho back in what may be Bilić's strongest side. Watford play a very weakened eleven with one eye on the weekend's FA Cup semi-final, though we do get to see former Swiss high-roller Valon Behrami back at the Boleyn – a man billed as 'the Swiss David Beckham' until he came to us.

West Ham take the lead after eleven minutes, when Payet lofts a precise ball over the Watford defence and Andy Carroll prods home with his left foot. That's Carroll's sixth goal in six games and his ninth of the season. If he can score a few more in the remaining four games he might get noticed again by Roy Hodgson.

Nigel, working late again, arrives after the goal, just as Watford have a decent spell and Adrián has to make a smart stop from Jurado. It's also great to have a minute's applause for former Hammer Dylan Tombides in the thirty-eighth minute, on the second anniversary of his death.

West Ham's nerves are calmed on half-time when ref Mike

Dean awards a softish penalty, ruling that Kouyaté was held down as he jumped in the box. Mark Noble does the rest.

At half-time, Michael again spots our Time Lord mate Donald Sumpter, though we think he might be avoiding his Whovian stalkers.

We get another penalty as Antonio surges between three defenders and is pulled down. Noble puts it straight down the middle and scores. Gomes might have saved two penalties from West Brom's Berahino in his last game, but not from Nobes.

It's a strange game and has more of the air of a testimonial as Lanzini misses a great chance and West Ham try to walk the ball into the net. 'Maybe Adrián will run down the pitch and score,' suggests Lisa.

West Ham look tired and it's a mystery why Bilić doesn't bring on some fresh legs earlier as Watford pull back a goal through a fine-hooked effort from Prödl. Cresswell and Payet try their best to create a fourth as the game looks like ending in an easy home win. The Bobby Moore Stand go through their greatest hits of Luděk Mikloško and Christian Dailly ditties. In the final minute, Watford earn a penalty for an innocuous-looking challenge by Ogbonna. Troy Deeney takes it, but Adrián saves to great cheers. And there's still time for Watford's Amrabat to be sent off after a second yellow card.

So it's off to the Central after a welcome three points. That was our fifteenth home league game without defeat, a Premier League record. 'Just when we've finally turned Upton Park into a Fortress, we're moving,' muses Fraser. Wonder if we can return the Olympic Stadium to sender?

Nigel's been to see former Status Quo drummer John Coghlan at the Half Moon in Putney and has missed the revelation that Michael plans to dye his hair claret and blue for the Man United game. He's less impressed with Michael's proposed Marc Almond musical. So I suggest an Andy Carroll musical of high drama and romance featuring Billi Mucklow, goals, parties and pink bedrooms. Michael thinks it might need a good understudy in the event of injury to the star performer.

The loud music comes on as the dodgy DVD seller does her rounds, so we head home. 'That's our last-ever victory against a team from the south of England,' muses Nigel as we walk past the fine old vista of a floodlit Boleyn Ground viewed from Barking Road.

A welcome three points after four draws, even if Man United and Liverpool have both won. But West Ham have a five-point lead over Southampton and can now really make a bid to finish in the top six.

It's a good week for Mark Noble. Four goals and now the *Evening Standard* reveals that Noble and ex-Hammers

Bobby Zamora and Rio Ferdinand, who all grew up on council estates, have teamed up to form the Legacy Foundation, which aims to encourage developers to build communities of mixed private-rented and public housing with sports facilities for kids. Nobes, who, as the song says, comes from Canning Town, recalls 'moving house seven times in four years when I was in social housing in Newham'. All three seem to be genuinely interested in the project rather than simply fronting it. Is it too late to vote for Mark Noble as Mayor of London?

West Brom away is next and the Irons make sure they won't be the victim of any dodgy decisions by winning 3-0. West Brom might have little to play for, but they have drawn at title-chasing Spurs on Monday and it's never easy to play against a Tony Pulis team of giant centre-backs. West Ham owe a debt to Ogbonna for a brilliant goal-line clearance in the early stages when WBA dominate. But two first-half goals kill the game off. Payet – who else? – makes the cross for Cheikhou Kouyaté's headed opener and Noble pokes home the second in a classic breakaway goal created by the speed of Kouyaté on the left.

The third goal is a brilliant volley from Noble after Payet

glides through the midfield and Andy Carroll lofts in a delicate cross. The ball crashes into the roof of the net. Goal machine Noble now has four goals in two games and it's a long time since we've won an away game so comfortably.

West Ham go fifth on Saturday night and that's ten games unbeaten in the Premier League – a club record. We've also achieved a record Premier League points total. And surely the Irons will beat Swansea in our penultimate home game.

The following Monday, Leicester City win the league after Spurs can only draw 2-2 at Chelsea, which gives hope to us all. Poor old Spurs…

Saturday 7 May arrives and the supporters gather for what was originally scheduled to be West Ham's final home game. Green Street is full of nostalgic fans with cameras photographing the John Lyall gates for our last Saturday match at the Boleyn. As it's so hot, I'm wearing my short-sleeved 1960s West Ham shirt with a v-shaped collar, which previously resulted in a 2-1 home defeat to Spurs. Could this be a mistake?

First off it's a visit to the Newham Bookshop to leave signed copies of my books *Hammers in the Heart* and *Irons in the Soul* for a Belgian fan. Then it's on to the huge queue at Ken's Café, where all the glory-hunters who have read my blog on Carol and Ken are wanting a taste of Ken's chips. In the queue I take phone orders from Lisa, Matt and Michael

British Heart Foundation
49 Hertford Street
Coventry
West Midlands
CV1 1LB

Branch No: 016
Telephone: 024 7622 7920

Charity Reg. No England & Wales (225971)
Charity Reg. No Scotland (SC039426)
Vat Registration No. 626 931 824

841876 07/03/2017 15:01

You were served by DONNA

Fiction Books
1x 3.50 3.50 Z
Gift Aid Donor ID: 9294271

TOTAL ITEMS 1 3.50

£4.00
£0.50

IN ABOVE TOTAL AMOUNT

0.00 IN 3.50

Thank you for shopping with us today.
Through your support, you have
made a difference to the fight against
heart disease.
Please keep your receipt as proof of
purchase.

NEED TO BRING SOMETHING BACK?

Changed Your Mind?
We exchange or refund items returned in their original condition within 28 days of purchase, with the original BHF ticket attached and a valid receipt.
Items excluded from this policy:
CDs, DVDS, Videos, Computer Games, Books, Earrings, Headwear, Underwear, Swimwear.

Not Happy with Your Purchase?
If the product you purchase is not of a satisfactory quality, not as described or not fit for its purpose, we may offer an exchange or refund, in accordance with your consumer rights. Be aware that many of our items are second hand and may have imperfections.

We reserve the right to refuse a return or to require proof of identity. Your Consumer rights are not affected.
Refunds will be made on the same tender type for cash or card, as the purchase.

Here to Help: customerservice@bhf.org.uk
Freephone - 0800 138 6556

for various combinations of cheesy chips and big breakfasts with no chips but an extra egg and lightly sautéed mushrooms. Someday there will be an app for this.

An unknown Swansea fan in the café thanks me for writing *Hammers in the Heart*, which is a nice surprise. Nicola Branch, a West Ham supporter and Hillsborough campaigner, arrives in her West Ham shirt but minus a ticket. Amazingly, she does eventually get one from the box office. DC arrives with his wee men and instead of his usual cameo performs a veritable three-act play as he stops for at least five minutes for souvenir pics of the team that meets in caffs.

Then Michael presents Carol with a bottle of the finest wine known to humanity. She looks touched and Michael is rewarded with a rare appearance from Ken himself and a photo opportunity with Carol and Ken.

On to the stadium. After a hearty 'Bubbles' from the shirt-sleeved crowd, West Ham start off as if it's going to be a stroll. The whole ground is in a party mood and on the Bobby Moore Stand a banner pays tribute to the Green Man, E6. Next to it stand several geezers in surfing shirts with another banner saluting 'Hawaiian Hammers – We'll wear what we want'. Everyone's singing 'We're all having a party – 'cos Tottenham f**ked it up!'

Early on Payet puts a free kick onto the roof of the net and Lanzini has a good shot tipped away by Fabiański. But Ki is getting a lot of space on the left and West Ham start to look strangely lethargic. After twenty-five minutes, Antonio loses the ball and is caught out of position. Ki crosses to Naughton on the other flank, Cresswell is missing and from the cross an offside Routledge taps home, having lost our centre-backs. That's a dampener.

Six minutes later, full-back Kingsley powers past a static Moses. Antonio doesn't close him down and from Kingsley's superb cross, Ayew is quicker than Ogbonna and Reid and flicks it home. A sudden silence descends over Upton Park as the Swansea fans sing 'Land of My Fathers' and then, 'Are you Villa in disguise?'

Our struggles are summed up as Carroll fires across the box and Lanzini shoots over the bar from a foot out while lying on the ground.

At half-time, 'Start Me Up' comes on the PA, with its apt refrain of 'You'll make a grown man cry!' On the East Stand, concourse actor Donald Sumpter is behind us texting for help from the High Council of the Time Lords. Matt, who has been marooned in Row Q for the first half, launches a long diatribe at the hapless Victor Moses and Bilić for not starting with Sakho.

We're 3-0 down after fifty-one minutes as Barrow skins Antonio and crosses for the unmarked Ki to fire home first-time. Matt the Vicar's Son, now back next to us in a vacant seat, concedes that perhaps he was wrong to ridicule my suggestion of shoring up the defence by bringing on Tomkins at right-back. Nigel suggests we'll struggle to get a point. Swansea are playing really well and look more like the side of two seasons ago.

The pitch is still awash with party detritus. 'We need to get that big fat balloon off the pitch,' says Matt.

'But Nolan's already left,' quips Fraser.

There's a brief flurry as Antonio has a shot saved and Carroll fires just wide. But it's been a very strange West Ham performance; Antonio is not a natural defender, Lanzini has had a nightmare, Kouyaté looks clumsy, Noble has been anonymous, Carroll isn't dominating the defence and even Payet is toiling.

We pull a goal back as Payet crosses and Antonio (who has looked good going forward) has a header saved by Fabiański. In the resulting melee, sub Sakho appears to prod home, though Swansea's Kingsley is credited with the last touch.

Bizarrely, Bilić refuses to bring on Tomkins and push Antonio further up the pitch, and Swansea's fourth sums up our afternoon. From a West Ham corner, Andy Carroll turns with all the speed of the world's largest cruise liner and is dispossessed. Swansea break with two players against the retreating Mark Noble and after a swift one-two Gomis nets and runs to the away fans doing his silly crawling celebration.

The only consolation is that our party has agreed to go to a very packed Black Lion. As we pass No. 664 Barking Road, Nigel repeats his Iron Maiden joke that it belongs to 'the neighbour of the beast' at No. 666. Thankfully, it's the last Saturday he'll ever do this.

Still, perhaps the sound of boos at Upton Park and a rumbling sense of disappointment are a more fitting historical tribute to most of our years spent at the Boleyn, rather than the anticipated tonking of the Welshmen.

It takes for ever to get served in the sweaty back bar of the Black Lion, but at least the Doom Bar is good as we discuss the election and Michael's planned claret-and-blue rinse – anything other than the match. Bilić has it right when he says we didn't perform off the ball and had too many passengers. You can't just turn up and expect to win a Premier League game without working.

After ten matches unbeaten, West Ham forgot the basics. We can only hope for a proper final home performance against Man United on Tuesday.

16

THE FINAL FAREWELL

MIST HANGS IN THE AIR AND A THIN DRIZZLE FALLS OVER London. It's as if the heavens are crying for the Boleyn. As we wake up, Trevor Brooking is being interviewed on Radio 4's *Today*.

At breakfast Lola is wearing my old 1979 Admiral West Ham shirt to college as a tribute. She's a little tearful. 'Today will be a difficult day. Tomorrow will be better,' I tell her, paraphrasing a line from the children's book *Lilly's Purple Plastic Purse*.

'I know you've got other things on your mind, but could you sign this?' says Nicola, handing me a card for her friend Nicky's birthday. She keeps saying things like, 'I know this is a difficult day for you.' No, no, it's just a lump of concrete and steel, that's all.

Farewell pieces on the Boleyn Ground are everywhere. There's an artistic slow-motion BBC video of some iconic Green Street sites (including Ken's Café); *The Observer* has two pages of memories from the likes of Stevie Bacon and Tony Cottee; Saturday's *Guardian* has a great piece by Owen Gibson that reveals how poorly the local traders have been treated (surely they should all be granted licences at the Olympic Park?).

While the *Daily Telegraph* has a double-page feature talking to many of the usual suspects: Nathan's pie and mash shop, Gary Firmager and his stepladder, the West Ham Supporters' Club, the Tonkins brothers who run the two-for-one sweet stall and the nuns at Our Lady of Compassion church on Green Street.

The *Telegraph* piece concludes: 'So, it is a fundamental ambivalence that will frame Tuesday's curtain-call, an uncertainty that for all the financial benefits the Olympic Park might bestow, a large section of the community is losing its hub, its spiritual heart.'

I do some work at my computer, but it's hard to concentrate. In the last few days, the Farewell Boleyn marketing has accelerated; my inbox reveals West Ham are offering us our plastic seats in a box for £50, or, to use the marketing speak, 'your very own place in history'. There's also a 'historic watch' from the Ironworks Collection, price: £119, plus farewell shirts, scarves, hoodies, bags, inflatable hammers, mugs, top trumps and probably some of Arthur Daley's Taiwanese alarm clocks. You know the club has to be run as a business, but the relentless selling-off of our history has become a little dispiriting.

By the afternoon, there's a dress code decision to make. My short-sleeve 1960s shirt didn't work against Swansea in the sweltering heat; it's still humid but a little cooler today, so I'm pleased to revert to my undisputedly luckier blue away shirt with claret hoops.

So it's one last trip on the Hammersmith and City Line to Upton Park. The back page of the *Evening Standard* has a huge picture of Bobby Moore running out of the players' tunnel. Inside, another five pages are devoted to memories of the Boleyn Ground, with Ken Dyer recalling how as a child he was passed over dockers' heads to the front of the Chicken Run and Mark Noble and Trevor Brooking discussing what it takes to play at Upton Park.

Green Street is full of fans with cameras during my walk to the Newham Bookshop at 5 p.m. A large crowd of fans is singing 'We've got Payet!' round the World Cup statue and the word is they've been drinking since noon. The statue of Bobby Moore has a claret-and-blue scarf round his neck. Vivian and John are dispensing bottles of pale ale to the favoured. I sign two of my books for one of the Belgian Irons, a lecturer called Ivan from Antwerp. Then a fan from Sweden says he's enjoyed them too and my suggestion is that Britain must surely remain in the EU to maintain these Newham/Europe links.

It's on to Ken's Café for a final egg, chips and beans, bread and butter and cup of tea. As promised, Michael has decided to add some literal colour to my blog by dying his hair claret and blue. Even more controversially, he's wearing a shirt with Jonathan Spector's name on the back (which is liked by Mrs Spector on Twitter). Matt's there, minus his unlucky Dukla Prague away shirt but in an early 1960s WHU top, along with claret-clad Lisa, who's got a ticket from DC (who stops to eat, so momentous is the occasion). Nigel is in his claret-hooped away shirt for 'the London derby' against MUFC.

Big Joe arrives with Candy on a romantic dinner date while Phill Jupitus eats one last isotonic liver, bacon and mash. He recommends some good museums for next Sunday's trip to Stoke, scarpering before Carol sees that he's not finished his mash. As we leave for the match, Carol dispenses kisses to us all, which is very touching.

Walking past the bus station to the East Stand, Matt and Nigel recycle their papers behind the away coaches and, in a first-world, middle-class fan dilemma, wonder where the recycling facilities will be at Stratford.

Inside the East Stand, we find free T-shirts, wrist bands

and flag cards on our seats. Though Fraser refuses to compromise his mid-period Dexys look by wearing the shirt over his claret-and-blue neckerchief.

'It's all gone so quickly,' muses Nigel. 'A few weeks ago you looked at the fixtures and it seemed like it was still ages away.'

News comes through that the kick-off has been postponed until 8.30 p.m. because the Man United coach has been bottled. Lisa, trying to get into the Betway Stand, texts to say that it's chaos in Green Street. I start to envisage FA bans and playing behind closed doors at the new stadium next season. The coach attack is inexcusable and stupid and is surely the result of people without tickets drinking all day. Though, as David Sullivan says, why couldn't United have arrived earlier instead of close to 7 p.m.? Everyone knew there would be huge crowds and traffic congestion. It also seems the police have lost control of the large numbers of fans. The bottle-throwing is deplorable, but an early arrival would have minimised the security risks. My MUFC friend Robert texts to ask if it's an ICF reunion.

So the DJ has another forty-five minutes to fill, which tests his CD box, though Nigel is pleased when 'Iron Man' by Black Sabbath comes on, presumably borrowed from Slaven's personal collection. We get 'My Way' with a video, but no sign of Fraser's legendary version of 'Bubbles' by Frank Sinatra.

The sister of the bloke from the Treasury in front of us

asks for a picture and reveals that we are known as 'The Philosophers' to her party. Must be Matt's Socratic dialogues on Mark Clattenburg.

A brass band makes a reappearance at Upton Park for the first time since the 1970s (my dad would have enjoyed that) and plays a moving 'Abide with Me' as pictures of our late stars are flashed up.

At kick-off, there's a hugely emotional 'Bubbles', with the crowd divided into claret and blue blocks through wearing the free T-shirts. The misty, damp night adds to the atmosphere. It's the loudest I've heard a West Ham crowd, beating the atmosphere of Ipswich in the play-off semi-final and the Cup Winners' Cup game against Eintracht Frankfurt.

Suddenly a football match breaks out. West Ham show all the verve and commitment they were lacking against Swansea. Kouyaté has a great game as a defensive shield, with Noble more advanced. The Boleyn erupts after ten minutes as Cresswell finds Lanzini on the left and his pull-back is slotted into the corner by Sakho, with the aid of a deflection off Blind. 'DIAFRA SAKHO, HE SCORES WHEN HE WANTS!' roars the entire stadium.

The geezer behind us is an old-school fan wanting Bonzo to 'effing well sort out wanker Rooney, before politely asking Michael why he's wearing a Spector shirt. Wayne Rooney also gets taunted about grandmothers.

West Ham have two good chances as Andy Carroll goes through in a one-on-one, only to see his shot saved by de Gea and Payet curls a good chance wide. At half-time, we wonder if not getting the second might be costly.

Down in the concourse, Michael the Whovian finally gains courage (fortified by a few beers in the Boleyn) to ask for a photograph with actor Donald Sumpter, aka Lord High President of the Time Lords and also a young captain in *The Sea Devils*. Donald obliges. I nervously press the camera button for him. It doesn't get better than this.

United appear galvanised in the second half and begin well. The Bobby Moore Stand refuse to give the ball back to de Gea and the delay seems to affect West Ham's concentration. Mata skips past Ogbonna in the box and crosses for Martial to equalise. De Gea celebrates and gets a water bottle thrown at him and a not-very-witty East End chorus of 'You Spanish c**t!'

Carroll has a header cleared off the line but after seventy-two minutes United appear to have won it as Martial runs at Reid and scores from a seemingly impossible angle, beating Randolph at his near post.

But the crowd responds with a deep-throated roar of 'Come on you Irons!' Sinews are strained, Mark Noble is everywhere and some kind of psycho-kinetic vortex, possibly inspired by Donald Sumpter, is sucking the ball towards the United goal.

Mystic Matt is just saying that Antonio doesn't get headers anymore. Dimitri Payet hits a free kick into the wall, but given a second chance from the rebound he chips a lovely ball into the box for Antonio to rise and power a header into the top of the net and Upton Park erupts once more.

Should we respect the point? Surely it can't be a Hollywood ending? But there are seemingly higher powers at work here, and not just Andy Carroll.

Noble is hacked down again and from Payet's free-kick Winston Reid, seemingly in slow motion, heads into the net. De Gea gets a hand to it but can't prevent the ball spinning over the line. Winston runs for the corner before being engulfed by his teammates as there's another mass outpouring of elation among the claret-and-blue hordes. Who put the ball in the Mancs' net? Winston, Winston Reid.

West Ham threaten a fourth as the whole ground wills the Hammers home. We survive four minutes of added time and tumultuous cheers at the whistle nearly bring down the East Stand earlier than scheduled. We go sixth, which has been almost forgotten amid the mayhem.

Phew. The players return for a lap of honour complete with Adrián holding his baby and lots of mini Dimitris. Then it's 'Twist and Shout' and 'Hi Ho Silver Lining' as a stage is erected, possibly for Two Bob Ray and Smooth Steve from the Central.

In a way, after an evening like that, I'd just like the game itself to stand as a memorial to the Boleyn.

But after Sugar Hut-style lights, flames and fireworks, the closing ceremony begins, compèred by Sky Sports' Bianca Westwood and Ben Shephard, though it should have been Jeremy Nicholas, our old announcer. Bianca talks to Carlton Cole and Marlon Harwood, who both get some songs from the stands, but it's all a bit over-stretched.

The videos and Olympic opening ceremony-style taxis (was Alan Dickens driving one?) bringing in the former Hammers stars aren't really necessary and perhaps they should just have stuck to Brooking, Di Canio, Martin Peters and Mark Noble. Bizarrely, there's no mention of Geoff Hurst either, and Bonzo can't make it, though Nigel gives Pottsy a standing ovation.

Still, Paolo gets it right by mentioning loyalty and passion and Mark Noble gets huge cheers for declaring: 'I've got my family here. I mean every West Ham fan out there when I say my family. Thanks to every single one of you.'

Leicester might have got the Italian tenor singing 'Nessun Dorma', but our evening ends with the Cockney Rejects performing 'Bubbles'. Just as well that they don't do 'West Side Boys' or 'War on the Terraces' after the coach incident.

The video screens show a figure in a number six shirt flicking a switch. As the lights go out, announcing 'Mr Moon has left the stadium' is a lovely touch at the end.

It's 11.30 p.m. Everyone has to rush for the last Tube, so no lingering last looks at Boleyn… We take one last visit to the Gents and ponder nicking the 'no solid objects in the urinal' sign, but think better of it. Fraser and Michael, in a triumph of optimism over experience, venture off to see if the Central is open.

Nigel, Matt and myself walk to East Ham. At the Tube, Matt goes off in search of Lisa, who's coming down the Barking Road, fans throng at the barriers and Nigel and I run down the stairs to catch the last Hammersmith and City Line train. It feels a little like the last helicopter out of Saigon. They'll probably be finding fans marooned in East Ham in ten years' time, still refusing to admit that the 2015/16 season is over.

It's a shame that a few Herberts outside will get all the headlines, but inside the stadium it's been a fitting tribute – exciting, exhausting, intimidating and thoroughly nerve-shredding. At one o'clock I finally make it home, and deprived of a last dodgy beer at the Central, head down to the cellar, break out a Bowmore whisky and toast our old friend – the Boleyn Ground.

17

WE'RE ALL GOING ON A EUROPEAN TOUR

DESPITE WEST HAM'S EPIC TRIUMPH OVER MAN UNITED, the papers focus on the cans and bottles thrown at the Man United coach. 'Boleyn farewell party turns sour' is the headline on *Guardian Sport*, with a picture of a tearful mother and child being escorted through the crowds by two West Ham fans as a smoke bomb goes off and the crossroads by the Boleyn starts to look like Aleppo. 'Life ban for the thugs who did this,' reads the back of the *Standard*, alongside a picture of bottles being lobbed at the coach. The match review is more positive: 'A night of drama and disaster that summed up Boleyn years', as Ken Dyer reports on a 'pulsating match'.

With some 10,000 ticketless fans outside the ground and many getting progressively drunker, there were always likely to be crowd-control problems. West Ham's co-chairman David Gold suggests that perhaps the scenes mean it's correct to move to Stratford: 'Upton Park is completely at its capacity; 35,000 is all that it can cope with. There were 45,000 fans there and it gridlocked the East End of London. What we had was tens of thousands of fans in the streets. You can't have that. Modern stadiums have all got overspill areas. Upton Park doesn't.'

In the Thursday *Guardian*, David Hytner writes a measured account of the incident, asking why the Safety Advisory Group that meets before the game didn't consider closing Green Street, why the Man United coach arrived so late and why it was allowed to go past the Boleyn pub. While the *Standard* has pictures of fans walking off with pilfered stadium signs.

There does need to be some sense of perspective. Throwing missiles at the coach was obviously wrong, but eyewitnesses suggest it only went on for a minute or two. An outer window of the coach was smashed but no one was injured and there was no fighting. It's interesting to note that when Liverpool later play in the Europa League Final there is actual fighting between Liverpool and Sevilla fans, which gets only a passing paragraph in most of the press.

Perhaps a bit of aggro reflects the fact that over the years Upton Park has not been that pleasant a visit for opposition fans and players. It used to be a rough, working-class place, where hooligans prospered in the 1970s and '80s and the rest of us tried to avoid trouble.

I'm surprised how bereft I feel by the loss of Upton Park. Did the Ancient Greeks feel like this when the Acropolis fell into ruins? Best not pursue that analogy too far, though, or I'll start to see Christian Dailly as a curly haired philosopher standing in front of the sacred columns of Athens.

It would be easy to over-sentimentalise leaving E13; most West Ham fans long ago moved out of Newham to Essex and the Home Counties. But returning to the Boleyn has symbolised people's roots and an old tight community that has now gone.

Meanwhile, it's a strange sensation to be going to Stoke when it feels like the season has ended and we're homeless. But away games at least prove that West Ham is a moveable feast. We're still West Ham even up in the Potteries. Perhaps West Ham United is more of a concept, a state of mind, than a club tied to a stadium. The 35,000 fans on Tuesday night made the Boleyn a cacophony of sound. When we add another 25,000 fans at the Olympic Stadium, the noise should be frightening, at least if the new roof does its job.

It's been a long season; we were initially at Upton Park in

July for the Europa League qualifiers. But at least next time round we'll be talking about firsts rather than every game being the last something or other. It's been an emotional marathon, but if we can go out on a win then Europa League football is guaranteed.

⚽ ⚽ ⚽

So, on the final Sunday of the season, it's off to Stoke on the 10.20 a.m. from Euston and a meeting with my second cousin Terry, who's secured tickets among the Stokies – my mum came from Stoke before meeting my dad (an Essex man). Terry, a lifelong Stoke fan, takes me to the Gardeners Retreat, where they serve a nice pint of Pedigree. But it's under new management and the crush at the bar resembles the Central. We purchase copies of the *Oatcake* fanzine and various Stoke fans in replica shirts reminisce about leaving the Victoria Ground. Matt doesn't make it to the Gardeners as, being a man of culture, he's looking at the pottery museum and art gallery in Hanley, as recommended by Phill Jupitus.

It's a lovely day and there's a rare sighting of the sun in Stoke as we head past the incinerator and over the motorway, across the reclaimed colliery site and up 'Cardiac Hill' to the Britannia, where David Gold's Roller is prominent in the car park. We're sitting among the Stoke fans next to the away section, where we have a fine view of the artistic patterns mowed onto the pitch by the groundsmen. You can see the hills of Stoke through the corner of the ground by the Boothen End and they look almost picturesque, in a post-industrial kind of way.

The home fans also seem very keen to tell West Ham 'you can stick your f**king bubbles up your arse!' The Hammers fans are busy having a party 'cos Tottenham f**ked it up. Though the bad news is Payet's out with an injury picked up against Man United.

Kouyaté immediately races down the wing to win a corner. Despite the absence of Payet, West Ham completely dominate the first-half against a pedestrian Stoke. The Hammers take the lead after twenty minutes as Reid gets his head onto Lanzini's corner and Antonio is allowed to turn and shoot past Given. Europa League, here we come. West Ham should get a second; Sakho chests down Antonio's cross but shoots wide and Kouyaté shoots over when well placed.

Meanwhile, news comes through that Man United's game with Bournemouth has been postponed after a bomb alert. Turns out it's a training device not cleared away by their equivalent of Mr Moon. Still, at least no fans from Manchester will be affected.

Antonio has been excellent on the wing and at the start of the second half he races down the right and presents a perfect cross for Sakho, who seems certain to score. Instead, he allows veteran Given to pull off a fine save and I wonder if that moment will prove crucial.

Hughes has had words with Stoke at half-time, and a determined run by Shawcross raises the crowd. Ten minutes into the second half, Imbula is allowed slightly too much space and fires home a low shot from outside the box. Perhaps Randolph should have done better.

West Ham still press for a winner, though Bilić surprisingly takes off Carroll and replaces him with Valencia, while Emenike replaces Sakho and the Stoke fans suggest, 'Andy Carroll, he's off to the bar!' News comes through that Spurs are getting thrashed at Newcastle and the West Ham fans are all having a party again when Tottenham f**ked it up and managed to finish below Arsenal, coming third in a two-horse race.

Adam nearly scores from the halfway line only to be thwarted by the alert Randolph. There's a tremendous flurry of pressure from a corner as Emenike and Antonio are foiled by two brilliant parries from Given on his line. Valencia heads a chance over the bar that Carroll might have scored and then gets in an overhead kick that Kouyaté heads goalwards. The ball is almost completely over the line, but Whelan somehow manages to clear. I start to think that, knowing football, Stoke will now score a winner, as we've done everything but score.

Two minutes from time, Stoke win a corner. Sub Diouf is unaccountably unmarked and powers home a header before doing a double somersault and running into the crowd. That should improve their lap of honour, but we really should have won this easily. 'It's the first time we've scored from a corner all season,' reveals Terry.

The Stoke fans chant 'You're not going on a European tour!', more suggestions about bubbles and 'You're f**king shit, you're f**king shit!' 'Delilah' booms out. Forgive me, West Ham, I just couldn't take any more.

The game ends after five minutes of added time and we're now relying on Man United beating Palace in the FA Cup and have snatched seventh place from the jaws of sixth. Southampton have ended their season with four successive victories to move above us. This season was perhaps West Ham's one chance to make the top six, or even top four, when we found ourselves with a world-class player and the top teams all underachieved. But it's still been a season that was better than anyone expected and I've been pleased to see us play today; after the Boleyn farewell, seeing the lads on the pitch was tangible proof that the club goes on.

So it's back to the station where I finally manage to meet Matt, who's witnessed a West Ham fan banging his dread-locks into the concrete wall of the stand after Sakho's miss.

Luckily, Matt has Roger Protz's programme notes on Stoke

and we walk to the *Titanic*-themed White Star pub (the *Titanic*'s captain came from Stoke) for a very palatable pint of Titanic plum porter, which is rather an apt brewer considering our European hopes might just have been holed. Matt reveals the pleasing fact that had we reached the FA Cup Final it would have been the longest season in Premier League history. It all started on 2 July against FC Lusitans. So now we're all going to have to support LVG's men on Saturday before we can finally relax.

The following Saturday, I go over to my Man United-supporting mate Robert's house to watch the final. Not living in Manchester, I feel entirely at home supporting United. It looks like we might be going to do a Spurs when Puncheon gives Palace the lead with twelve minutes to go. But thankfully Mata equalises. United's Smalling is sent off in extra time and again it looks like we're not going on a European tour. But United play better with ten men and Jesse Lingard fires home an unstoppable winner.

The Saturday night media concentrate on the fact that Louis van Gaal is on his way out and José Mourinho is going to Old Trafford, while missing the really big story – West Ham have made it to the third qualifying round of the Europa League.

West Ham have finished seventh and made it into Europe. And we've still got Payet. The Boleyn is soon to be bulldozed.

Will the Olympic Stadium be a soulless bowl or propel the club to become by far the greatest team the world has ever seen?

What will it be like visiting Upton Park when the Boleyn is replaced by executive housing? There's an auction coming up, but I'd prefer to remember the ground as it was, rather than being sold off by the metre.

Stratford beckons. New pre-match rituals will have to be initiated. It's goodbye to Ken's Café, the Central, the Black Lion, the Boleyn, the Queens, Belly Busters burger bar, the Stevie Baconburger stall, Ercan fish and chips, Nathan's pie and mash and numerous other Upton Park institutions. A new era begins, but we'll miss you, the Boleyn Ground.

18

OLYMPIAN HAMMERS

NOTHING MUCH HAPPENS OVER THE SUMMER.

Britain votes for Brexit after an acrimonious referendum. Prime Minister David Cameron resigns. Boris Johnson looks set to be the new Prime Minister until Michael Gove withdraws his support, resulting in numerous Brutus-inspired headlines. Theresa May eventually wins the contest to be the new Conservative Party leader and Prime Minister. In her instant reshuffle, Chancellor George Osborne and Secretary of State for Justice Michael Gove are sacked from the May Team. Meanwhile, 172 Labour MPs sign a vote of no-confidence in leader Jeremy Corbyn and most of the shadow Cabinet resign, despite Corbyn's mandate from the party members. Nigel Farage resigns as leader of UKIP.

Chris Evans joins in the resignation-mania by quitting *Top Gear*.

Back on planet football, Russian and English fans clash in Marseille and Roy Hodgson resigns after England's Brexit from the European Championships. England have somehow managed to lose to Iceland and at the final whistle commentator Guðmundur Benediktsson produces the most gloriously high-pitched, orgasmic commentary in history. Dimitri Payet stars for hosts France early on in the tournament, but ends up with only a runners-up medal as Portugal go on to win the final even though Ronaldo is injured, thanks to a goal scored by Swansea City reject Éder. Most surprising of all, Sam Allardyce is named as the new England manager – enough to have my pal Fraser spluttering into his post-match Carlsberg.

We've not had much time to mourn the Boleyn. We return from a family holiday in Glenridding, where Nicola, Nell, our border terrier Vulcan and I manage to scale Striding Edge on the way up to Helvellyn. This narrow edge of jagged rocks has claimed several lives in windy and snowy conditions, but thankfully we survive. In fact, it's not much more difficult than trying to clamber down from the back of the old East Stand to the gents. No sooner have we unpacked our walking poles, however, than football sweeps into focus.

Just nine weeks after the FA Cup Final, West Ham are back in action in the Europa League Third Qualifying Round on 28 July. The club has a new crest; a simple set of crossed hammers, but minus the Boleyn Castle. The word 'London' has been added underneath, as if to imply that there is only one team in London.

Slaven Bilić has signed Algerian winger Sofiane Feghouli, midfielder Hårvard Nordtveit, former Man United striker Ashley Fletcher and Beşiktaş winger Gökhan Töre on loan. Even so, West Ham lose 2-1 to Slovenian side NK Domžale in the away leg. Mark Noble converts a penalty for the Hammers but in their first competitive game of the season a strong but clearly not match-fit Hammers side loses to a side from a town with a population of just 12,000.

The return leg, a week later, will be West Ham's first game in the Olympic Stadium. It's been a rush to convert the stadium from the Anniversary Games athletics; West Ham had to apply for special UEFA dispensation to switch the dates of the home and away legs, having originally been drawn to play at home in the first leg.

The day before the Irons' debut at the Olympic Stadium, I visit the Boleyn Ground once more. A signal failure on the District Line reminds me how Upton Park is always vulnerable to delays. In Green Street, Ken's Café is shut up as Carol and Ken are on their holidays. Four drinkers sit in the front bar of the Boleyn. The West Ham pictures in the Ercan chip shop are now a sad reminder of the recent past. On a non-match day, it's more like Brentwood High Street than a thriving football metropolis.

The Boleyn Ground is looking moribund with the club sign and crests removed. The John Lyall gates have gone and are now boarded up with black wood. Groups of workmen in orange bibs dig up part of the car park as new owners Barratt conduct 'initial site surveys and archaeological works' – perhaps they'll find Billy Bonds's discarded shin pads. A letter sent to local residents from Barratt reveals that the Boleyn Ground will now be referred to as Upton Gardens. Barratt says it will be working around the 'memorial garden commemorating loved ones affiliated with West Ham United' and the area will be preserved and treated with respect.

Drybake Final Score Limited will be filming at the site from 8 August to 16 September. The movie *Final Score* will be a *Die Hard*-style thriller starring Pierce Brosnan. The plot involves a desperate group of men holding a 35,000-strong crowd hostage at a sports ground – which all sounds a bit like playing Wimbledon's crazy gang. The movie is set to end with Upton Park being partially blown up. I'd much rather the stadium is demolished behind closed doors and with a little dignity.

It's more cheering to visit the Newham Bookshop. Vivian and John offer me a drink and suggest an event to mark the publication of this book. Vivian says she's hopeful the flat-buyers in Upton Gardens might be book-buyers. A customer comes in with a request. 'We've had a bit of a run on Proust,' answers Vivian, words you don't normally associate with E13.

After a rather good lunchtime curry in the takeaway next to the Boleyn, I visit the Who Shop and buy *Doctor Who Magazine*, in which the great Tom Baker mentions both Bobby Moore and my fellow Hammer Michael the Whovian. Trade is still brisk among the Whovians and perhaps life goes on after West Ham in the Barking Road, even if the East Stand looks forlorn.

The Overground train home from Stratford goes past the Olympic Stadium and a series of giant letters are being erected. At present it reads 'st am United', but it's going to look impressive.

Thursday arrives with a feeling of nervousness similar to the last game at the Boleyn. What if it doesn't work and it's a soulless concrete bowl where you can't see the pitch? It's a hot day and after musing on the feasibility of a Philosophy

Football Blowing Bubbles T-shirt, I opt to go jacketless in my 1970s hooped away shirt.

The journey to Stratford on the Overground is certainly quicker than the old trek to Upton Park. Outside the Westfield exit, fans in replica shirts are looking slightly lost in the shopping centre. Heading up the escalators to the food mall, my evening starts with a black-bean burrito – strange how Ken's Café never extended to the Mexican market. Other West Ham fans are stocking up on protein at the Chicago Rib Shack – the franchise version of Upton Park's one-legged Rib Man.

Fraser has suggested we meet in the Tap East opposite Stratford International station. I'm not sure where this is and take a circuitous route via the imaginatively-named The Street, then Westfield Avenue and past a car park and over a bridge to Stratford International, ending up basically where I'd started out from. Fraser and Lisa are waiting in the Tap East, a modern bar with numerous craft beers. Lisa breaks the news that Joey O'Brien has been released. Despite a large crowd, the bar staff serve us quickly and we enjoy a swift drink of specially named ales such as East End Mild, Boleyn Bitter and Number Six Blonde. The Central it ain't.

Finishing our pints, we walk down to the end of The Street and glimpse the vast London Stadium. The trek down Stratford Walk is undeniably exciting. It feels like a cup final and we're now playing at Wembley or the Millennium

Stadium every week. Shouts of 'Irons!' accompany the march of camera-wielding fans. Overpriced vending caravans line the route, though nothing as good as Ken's Café. The 'West Ham United' name on the stadium certainly looks imposing and the club has done a decent job with wraparound portraits of Mark Noble, Winston Reid and co. on the stadium. We stop for a souvenir picture before the new sign.

Yet, it also feels fantastically strange to be walking through a vast open space towards a football stadium. There are no cramped Victorian terraces, no cafés, no pubs on the corner. Everything is modern, concrete, corporate, landscaped – and we can see Canary Wharf and the towers of Docklands on the horizon. The strange mangled shape of Sir Anish Kapoor's ArcelorMittal Orbit sculpture stands next to the stadium, looking like the Eiffel Tower after a particularly heavy tackle from Julian Dicks.

The *Evening Standard* writes: 'The club has undergone one of the most dramatic and instant character changes of any organisation in the history of English football.' It's progress perhaps, but still a shock, and everyone looks a little bewildered by the occasion.

Earlier in the week, *The Guardian* reported that home-ownership had hit a thirty-year low in England. Now West Ham have also forsaken home-ownership to join Generation Rent, though our tenancy agreement does run for 100 years and our new gaff is convenient for John Lewis. No wonder the fans look confused by it all – we've moved from a terrace in Upton Park to the equivalent of a Billericay mansion with electric gates and falcons on the gateposts and a swimming pool round the back. But the mood is generally optimistic and the fans want it to succeed – most of West Ham's fans still come from Essex and they like a bit of stadium bling.

However, the programme-selling clearly needs working on. Huge queues have formed at every seller. Here we're met by Matt, who, ever since his Wigan away debacle, has always ensured he gets a programme two hours before kick-off. Tonight, Mystic Matt is wearing a black T-shirt as Fraser has banned him from wearing his 'lucky' Dukla Prague away shirt in the new stadium. Matt suggests trying the vendors further round, but everywhere has gigantic queues. After a twenty-minute wait I eventually get my souvenir edition with Mark Noble on the cover from a vendor who's running short of change, at which point Fraser quips could I go back and see if they've got Bournemouth at home from last season.

Entrance to the stadium is nice and speedy as, after a bag search, we place our tickets in an electronic turnstile and head through Gate H. Inside the gents a urinal is overflowing, with someone quipping, 'Some things don't change!' But it's much easier to find a loo now and to get served at the refreshment kiosks.

There's an immediate sense of relief upon finding our seats. We can see the pitch and there's lots of legroom, even if the dug-outs seem lightyears away on the far side and the playing area is much bigger than at the Boleyn. The new roof is partially transparent and means that everyone will stay dry and Slaven Bilić might not need his beanie hat anymore.

The green plastic covering over the athletics track looks a little garish, but is going to be replaced by AstroTurf – or possibly some leopard-skin carpet from Andy Carroll's gaff – and with 60,000 due for league games there should be a big noise. It could work.

Nigel's eschewed the chance to see the spiritual home of Iron Maiden in Stratford in favour of a holiday, while Michael the Whovian is on thespian duties, having earlier emailed to announce that, with Cresswell and Lanzini out and Tomkins sold, 'We're doomed, we're all doomed!'

Alison and Scott from Maldon have made it to the seats behind us. Alison has had to remortgage her house to buy a stadium Coke, but despite some initial reservations about the sun in her eyes two hours before kick-off, admits that under May's leadership we seem to have booked half-decent seats as we strive not to exit Europe.

Then it's 'Bubbles' time. It immediately sounds impressive in these cavernous surroundings and the new roof contains most of the sound. It's a strain on my contact lenses to see some of the action on the far side, but generally I can still make out the West Ham players' numbers and see the action.

West Ham make the perfect start after eight minutes, when Valencia does well to run at the defence and get in a cross, Byram scuffs his shot towards goal and Cheikhou Kouyaté back-heels home before running to the new Sir Trevor Brooking Stand to celebrate. It's quite a shock to see a working scoreboard and a replay of the goal.

Domžale look a decent-ish, if limited, side considering their meagre resources, but Reece Oxford makes some timely interceptions at the back, Nordtveit looks more at home as a defensive midfielder and Feghouli (which is pronounced 'Fehouli', says my Algerian barber) is busy on the right. Our full-backs are getting forward well and from Antonio's cross Andy Carroll cushions his header into the path of Kouyaté, who fires home his second. I text Michael the score and he replies: 'I never doubted you for a moment, Captain Bilić!'

We observe that, in the style of Arsenal at the Emirates, the club honours are listed on the front of the upper tier of the Betway Stand. It's just the four though: the FA Cups of 1964, 1975 and 1980 and the Cup Winners' Cup of 1965. 'Where's the Intertoto Cup?' asks an indignant Fraser. If we want to pad it out we could add the Division 2 titles of 1981 and 1958 and the play-off wins of 2005 and 2012, plus being runners-up in the 2006 FA Cup and the 1981 League Cup and 1976 Cup Winners' Cup. And winning the World Cup in 1966.

Quite a few 'If you 'ate Tottenham stand up!' and 'If you love West Ham stand up!' chants go round the stadium as the crowd start to feel at home. It's a little tentative, but the atmosphere is surely going to develop over time.

At half-time, we're joined by Steve from Cornwall, who's driven up to Ebbsfleet, then caught the train to the stadium, and plans to drive home after the game. We admit he might be a full-timer.

I suggest that the London derbies will be a big test of the atmosphere. 'We need to get Jermain Defoe here,' suggests Matt. 'Or bring Paul Ince out of retirement.'

There's a scare in the second half when Randolph has to save well from Ćrnic, but West Ham continue to press as Valencia and Feghouli both slice wide when through. The result is assured when Noble plays through Feghouli and this time the Algerian winger fires home with a crisp finish from the edge of the box. Feggy crosses his arms in a hammers gesture, kisses the turf and puts his shirt over his head, resulting in a booking from the jobsworth ref. Good celebration, though, suggesting he might become a bit of a cult figure.

Huge gaps in the white seats appear in front of us as the game nears its conclusion, which doesn't look good, though perhaps the part-timers know something about the journey time to the Tube. The Westfield route is closed and we're directed past the shopping centre and then stand kettled in the train queue before a *Blade Runner*-style skyline, as a brief chant goes up of 'We want the Boleyn back!'

Stewards with 'stop' and 'go' signs ensure steady progress, though there's another long wait on the bridge and a pushing match between two blokes before we escape, Steve McQueen-style, outside the Tube entrance to seek the pubs of Stratford, first walking through the old shopping centre, now frequented by a diaspora of skateboarders.

The Queen's Head is packed and the Secret Weapon denies us entry – 'So that's their secret weapon: no drinkers,' quips Fraser. Around the corner we opt for the Refreshment Room, which has three real ales and a decent beer garden. But it's taken 35 minutes to get here and there surely has to be a quicker route. Perhaps we'll experiment with Stratford International or Hackney Wick next time.

Almost forgotten in the history-making is that we've reached the next round of the Europa League, as Fraser reminisces about dodgy police in Sicily when we played at Palermo in the UEFA Cup.

Morale seems relatively good among the drinkers. The 'London Stadium' will never be as intimate as Upton Park, but 'Bubbles' still sounded great at the kick-off and once we've played a few games against the bigger clubs the ambience will grow. This was, after all, a game against the equivalent of a League One side. We could see the action pretty well from half-way back in the East Stand and while the fans are getting used to the stadium, as are the players, there were signs of an atmosphere developing by the second half. Club and fans are adapting to their new environment, but after such a quick turnaround from the athletics, this first night feels like a successful start to West Ham's new history. Remember all those predictions of empty seats? We've just played in front of a record crowd of 53,914 fans.

Three days later, London is calling again, as West Ham play Juventus in the Betway Cup – though really it's a pre-season friendly. This was originally intended to be the first game at the new stadium and we've paid an over-priced £35 for tickets. However, it's still another chance to acclimatise to our new home before the league begins.

This time I take my elder daughter Lola, soon to move to Paris for her gap year. We take an experimental journey on the Overground to Hackney Wick. At least there are some old warehouses by the station and there's more of a sense of an industrial heritage here. Lola's impressed by the hipster quotient outside the trendy bars.

Walking from the Overground is easy enough, as we amble past the Copper Box Arena and then up the wide expanse of London Way. By the stadium we find the sculpture of a giant bell, which has already led to a few Facebook jokes about the Betway Stand being the Bell End. The bell is inscribed with Shakespeare's lines from *The Tempest*: 'Do not be afeard, the isle is full of noises.' Well, Shakespeare did come from Stratford…

The stalls outside the ground are predictably expensive, and we pay £6 for a pasty and £3 for potato wedges. But the branding is looking good and an hour before kick-off fans are posing before the crossed hammers and 'We've got Payet' murals on the stadium exterior. Inside, giant shirts with the names of famous players are hanging from the girders, though it does appear as if Bobby Moore is now sponsoring the gents.

Inside the stadium each seat has a 'commemorative plastic bag' that we hold up at kick-off to make a giant 'Come on you Irons'. Matt, Lisa and Michael the Renaissance Fan are with us, with Michael pleasantly surprised by the stadium on his first visit. Lola gets a little emotional when the Bobby Moore video comes on and says she wants the Boleyn back.

The opening ceremony sees white-clad dancers holding up large letters spelling out the names of the stands and then, 'Thank you, founders.' Giant claret-and-blue and Oxford blue

Thames Ironworks shirts appear on the pitch. Then there's lots of flames and fireworks and a woman singing 'God Save the Queen' (not the Sex Pistols' version).

West Ham are wearing another new third kit, this time it's an all-black (or Oxford blue to use its correct name) outfit with a Union Jack on the chest. It's not, as one Twitter joker claimed, a bid for the Britain First market, but a tribute to the first kit worn by Thames Ironworks FC in 1895. Social media suggests that in their dark polo shirts the West Ham lads look a little like staff at the bookies or the geezers guarding the doors to the Boleyn.

It's difficult to read too much into the game as it's essentially a pre-season friendly and with unlimited subs both teams change virtually their entire starting elevens. But it's a pleasure to see stars such as legendary goalkeeper Buffon, Dani Alves, Dybala and latterly Higuaín and Chiellini. Matt reveals that he last saw Buffon give away a rubbish goal for Italy Under-21s at Bristol City in 1988 – not that he remembers every game…

Juventus play some really nice passing football early on and after Valencia hits the post, the Italians go ahead through the impressive Dybala. Winston Reid slips for the second as Mandžukić finishes well.

'We can't lose our own cup!' says Lola at 0-2 down.

'Well, we might get runners-up medals,' I suggest.

Should we make a comeback, we wonder if the Betway Cup will be added to the list of four honours on the Betway Stand.

However, better news for the Irons is that Andy Carroll is looking sharp. Byram gets in a good cross from the left and Carroll powers in a header. Buffon make a great save to push the ball against the post, but Andy is quick enough to beat a defender and poke home the rebound on the line.

At half-time we retreat to the concourse, where Lola and Michael discuss the musical *Hamilton* and Matt wonders why there's a musical about UKIP's leader in Wales. Crowd-wise, everyone seems happier now they know how to enter the ground and where to sit. Football fans are creatures of habit and need to feel relaxed in their new environs. Certainly in the new Bobby Moore Stand there are signs of more spontaneous chanting.

The second half sees many changes and substitute James Collins raises the crowd with some timely clearances. West Ham gain a free kick on the right and from Noble's cross Andy Carroll takes out four men, including two of his own side, to score with another thumping header. He looks happy with that one, punching the air, even if it is a friendly.

The dream is back on. A bewildering number of substitutions follow, but it's good to see the likes of Reece Burke, Josh Cullen, Marcus Browne, Martin Samuelsen, Ashley Fletcher and the lively Domingos Quina get work-outs. Though the biggest cheer is reserved for sub Dimitri Payet, with fifteen minutes to go. When 'We've got Payet!' rings round the stadium, there's some hope for a real atmosphere developing for future games.

Ginger Pelé gets a huge cheer for tackling Higuaín, meaning James is worth at least £100 million. But Juventus still continue to threaten and Simone Zaza hits the winner with five minutes left after the West Ham defence fails to counter a high ball.

We stay to see the Betway Cup presented to Gianluigi Buffon. 'He might have won the World Cup, but the Betway Cup is the big one,' suggests Matt.

The walk back to Hackney Wick is easy and without any queues, though we discover that the Number 90 bar doesn't admit anyone in football shirts. The hipster bar Grow with its waterside terrace is more inviting for future visits. The station is surprisingly crowd-free, the waiting room is air-conditioned and we even get a seat on the Overground. The journey to Highbury and Islington is so easy that there is surely hope of nicking a few Arsenal fans.

West Ham might have lost our first Cup Final of the season, but it's been a fairly relaxed afternoon in the sun. Soon the real stuff begins.

Before the first Premier League fixture, West Ham add three more players to the squad. French left-back Arthur Masuaku is signed from Olympiacos to replace the injured Cresswell, while Argentine striker Jonathan Calleri arrives on a year-long loan.

The big signing, though, is striker André Ayew from Swansea for £20.5 million. It's a bit worrying when a player who scores twelve goals in a season is worth that kind of money, though in the age of £89 million Paul Pogba, just signed by Man United, that's probably the going rate. He's undoubtedly a good finisher and provided quite a few assists from out wide too. Ayew has sixty-seven caps for Ghana and earlier in his career had a proven scoring record at Marseille. He's not the A-list striker the club were talking about at the start of the summer, but, at twenty-six, André should be coming into his peak years.

On the first Monday night of the season, West Ham lose 2-1 at Chelsea. It's all a little worrying. Chelsea look re-motivated by new boss Conte, while West Ham's midfield looks off the pace and star signing Ayew limps off after thirty-five minutes. Antonio, still played out of position at right-back, gives away a penalty after trying to dribble the ball out of his own box. It's only when Payet, rested after his exertions in France, comes on as a late sub that West Ham threaten. From Dimitri's corner, Collins's initial header ricochets off

Valencia and back into the path of the Ginger Pelé, who lashes the ball home, much to the glee of the away fans. It's our first shot on target. The Irons look like sneaking a point until one minute from time, when Captain Haddock lookalike Diego Costa is given too much time just outside the box and fires a low shot into the net. The ball goes through Collins's legs, but it wasn't right in the corner and perhaps the otherwise excellent Adrián might have got a hand to it. Chelsea gaffer Conte showboats by leaping into the crowd. To make it worse, Costa should earlier have received a second yellow card for going in late on Adrián.

Two days later comes the news that £20.5 million André Ayew is out for four months. It seemed a fairly innocuous thigh strain back on Monday night. Presumably André had a normal pre-season at Swansea, so it just seems a case of very bad luck. I'm reminded of the time Kieron Dyer joined us for £6 million in 2007 and immediately got crocked at Bristol Rovers – though hopefully André will make a much better long-term recovery than Kieron.

The Hammers have another Europa League game on Thursday night, drawing 1-1 at FC Astra Giurgiu. It's not that bad a result considering Slaven plays a weakened side, but again the Hammers have managed to throw away a better result. It all hinges on the eightieth minute when sub Marcus Browne does really well to beat the last defender and race clear down the left, before squaring to Antonio. It looks like Antonio, restored to his rightful position in midfield, has a tap-in. But somehow he manages to stroke the ball into the side netting. Even the best can miss easy chances, but to exacerbate that error Astra equalise a minute later. From a corner, Alibec (who, according to Matt's incendiary text, is 'a 20-stone pub player') manages to turn Collins and fire into the roof of the net.

Some things don't change with a new stadium. It's reassuring to read my old pal Steve 'North Bank Norman' Rapport's Facebook comment: 'Un-f**king-believable. Every single week, every single game we give away a late goal. EVERY GAME.' He's been saying that for forty years.

Meanwhile, the home match with Bournemouth will not be played before the planned 60,000 fans. The London Stadium Safety Advisory Group and Newham Council have restricted the capacity to just (*just?*) 57,000, claiming there was dangerous standing by some fans at the previous two games. The authorities might have been a bit more lenient, as we're trying to avoid a sanitised atmosphere and get some songs going. Long term, there's surely a case for the Premier League to allow small, safe standing areas, as in the German

Bundesliga. It must be annoying if you want to sit down and find yourself lumped with people standing up all game, and perhaps part of the problem is that the club has mixed up families and new ticket holders with the old diehards from the Bobby Moore Stand. Though standing up doesn't feel that dangerous with all the new legroom. But it seems we'll have to sit down if we love West Ham and get the capacity up to 60,000 before we can really go wild and stand up if we hate Tottenham.

So there's an injury crisis, a crocked record signing, a fixture pile-up, fans in trouble with the authorities and the club relying on Andy Carroll staying fit. It's almost like we've never left the Boleyn.

19

LONDON CALLING

THE FIRST PREMIER LEAGUE FIXTURE AT THE LONDON Stadium (though most fans would prefer the old title of the Olympic Stadium) is played against Bournemouth on Sunday 21 August. Britain is enjoying another Olympic frenzy as the likes of Laura Trott, Jason Kenny, Mo Farah, Bradley Wiggins, Charlotte Dujardin, Max Whitlock, Andy Murray, Nicola Adams, Jade Jones, Adam Peaty and West Ham-supporting hockey star Susannah Townsend win gold after gold. It's a reminder that the London Stadium already has some history with the 2012 Olympic Games. Four years ago, I managed to watch a day of the Paralympics from what is now the East Stand. And now that £700 million stadium, nicknamed 'the Taxpayers' Dome' by critics, is West Ham's new home.

As pre-match preparation, I've taken Nicola on a fact-finding mission to the hipster bars of Hackney Wick the previous Friday night. We visit Crate, which has superb Moor beer brewed on the premises, and then Grow, with its beds of herbs growing on the canal side terrace. For the first time ever, she likes my football pubs and is now talking about hiring a paddleboard from the nearby Milk Float Café.

Sunday's 4 p.m. kick-off allows plenty of time for a tour of Stratford. Cutting through the Stratford Centre to the Broadway, I discover that the Best Café does a Ken's Café-style egg, chips and beans, bread and butter and a cup of tea for £5.80. Though sadly there's no shouting of numbers at the customers. But it does have wooden tables, a similar menu to Ken's and a number of West Ham fans having their lunch.

Then it's a journey down the Grove past the Wetherspoons' pub the Goose and on to Iron Maiden's old local, the Cart and Horses. I step inside to look at the tiny stage, which has a picture of the young Iron Maiden playing at the pub, enough to make Nigel combust with pleasure. From the Cart and Horses, I walk to the Railway on Leyton Road, an old Victorian pub marooned among highways and high-rises. It's packed with West Ham fans, stocks Doom Bar and has pie and mash and Mrs Flipper's burgers stalls in the beer garden, along with a claret-and-blue gazebo.

If nothing else, the new stadium is improving my knowledge of London's geography. Walking along Penny Brookes Street (named after Victorian surgeon William Penny Brookes, who helped inspire the modern Olympic Games) and past some rather soulless new flats, I find Stratford International and walk over the railway bridge to the stadium. What's noticeable is that fans now gather around the stadium an hour before kick-off, gazing up at it like extras from *Close Encounters of the Third Kind*. Other fans search for their names on the founders' bricks laid outside the ground.

Walking around the complete circumference of the stadium, it's undeniably impressive. On three sides it's surrounded by water, and the proximity of the River Lea gives it some East End credibility – though sadly football fans don't seem to be allowed anywhere near the water. The stadium store works well and you can walk in and out without queuing – unlike the old shop in Green Street.

Inside the stadium, Michael, Fraser and Matt are already seated. Michael announces that he's been to Ken's Café, only, in a Hardy-esque twist, to find it closed, as Ken and Carol are doing the catering for a music festival. But he did have a brief audience with the E13 legends, if not a big breakfast. He also reports that there's an RAF helicopter parked outside the Boleyn in preparation for the filming of *Final Score*. We wonder if Pierce Brosnan will soon be a regular in Ken's.

MJ, one of my Hammers in the Heart blog correspondents, has been to the Black Lion before the game and says it's only half an hour's walk away. Perhaps there's hope for some of our old venues.

Nigel's returned from cycling in Burgundy and behind us there's Alison, her nephew Joe with a pre-hipster beard and Steve from Cornwall, who decided at 1.30 a.m., after watching telly and reading H. G. Wells, that sleep was for wimps and drove up to London. We're close to someone from the old East Stand too: Nigel's old mate, 'the bloke from the Treasury', whom he bumped into at a Stranglers concert.

Initially I think Matt is joking when he says Andy Carroll is out for six weeks. But no, it's true; a long-term Andy Carroll injury is as sure a sign of football returning as half-and-half scarves, Mourinho mind games and Wenger parsimony. It seems Andy's done his knee in during a substitute appearance in Romania. We didn't even need to bring him on. His last big injury came after playing midweek at Southampton, so surely it would have been safer to rest him at Astra?

Payet is missing again, apparently with a slight knock. Matt worries that this means Dimitri's going to be sold. You wonder if Harry Redknapp will be returning, as we're already down to the bare bones: our squad is minus seven players in Cresswell, Lanzini, Payet, Ayew, Carroll, Feghouli and Sakho.

Thankfully, having had an eye test, my new set of contact

lenses means I have a better view of the action and scoreboard, even if it is still a giant cauldron of a stadium. My lenses are severely tested by Bournemouth's away kit, which is fluorescent green and makes them look like a team of cycle couriers.

Bournemouth's Adam Smith has a tame effort saved and Matt wonders if he was a free-market transfer.

'It's like he's being directed by an invisible hand,' I suggest.

The first half is memorable only for a decent Valencia effort saved by Boruc and for Nigel asking us to name the 1979 song that was a hit for the Charlie Daniels Band (no relation to the Bournemouth full-back). The answer is 'The Devil Went Down to Georgia'. For the Cherries, Jordan Ibe inexplicably opts not to shoot when through and a great shot by Joshua King is acrobatically tipped over the bar by Adrián.

The side work hard, with Masuaku and Byram solid at the back, but Noble and Kouyaté struggle to create much in the absence of Payet, Töre doesn't get quality crosses in and lone striker Valencia is outnumbered. The atmosphere is initially more raucous now it's a proper league match, and it helps to have away fans, even if they are chanting 'Is this the Emirates?'

As the game becomes poorer, it quietens, although it's easily forgotten that a mediocre half like this would also have left Upton Park underwhelmed. The roof doesn't contain the sound as well as we might have hoped and it's hard to get the whole ground singing in unison because the stadium's so big, but the sheer volume of 60,000 fans is at some stage going to make a lot of noise. A lot of fans have compared our 'migration' to the stresses of moving house, and when everything's out of cardboard boxes we'll all feel a lot better.

The number of fans drifting to the concourse ten minutes before the break gets a little irritating, though with 22,000 extra supporters we're always going to have a few more prawn sandwich-munchers. Those of us who attended the Boleyn can at least bask in the thought that we were there when we were shit – and sometimes quite good.

In the second half, it takes some heavy-handed stewarding down in the corner by the Bobby Moore Stand to rouse the crowd. The stewards are trying to force the more boisterous fans to sit down. Cue impassioned cries of 'We're West Ham United, we'll stand when we want!' as the stewards eject a persistent stander and it all threatens to kick off. This is becoming quite an issue and the stewards look more used to concerts than stroppy football crowds.

Mystic Michael suggests that Töre might be the next Ricardo Vaz Tê, a barbed comment that inspires our new young Turk. The game increases in intensity as Antonio crosses and Töre fires a difficult chance into the side netting. Antonio switches wings with Töre and our formation looks more effective. As Bournemouth make a substitution, James Collins risks a booking through trying to shove the tardy Jordan Ibe off the pitch and it gets big cheers.

Harry Arter (Scott Parker's brother-in-law) brings down Kouyaté after seventy-seven minutes and is sent off for a second yellow card. Finally, West Ham play with two strikers at home as Calleri and Fletcher come on. Some proper guttural chants of 'COME ON YOU IRONS!' emanate from the new Bobby Moore Stand and the decibel level is encouraging.

It looks like it might still end 0-0 until five minutes from time, when Antonio beats his full-back but over-hits the cross. Töre retrieves on the left, skilfully beats his man and stands up a superb cross for Antonio to rise above Charlie Daniels and head home. The isle really is full of strange noises as the fans celebrate the first league goal at the London Stadium and Antonio does a Macarena celebration. Good end to a difficult week for Michail, who's finally playing in his correct position.

'One-nil up against ten men. What could possibly go wrong?' asks Nigel.

The atmosphere is intense now and feels much more like a game at the Boleyn. As four minutes of added time arrives, Bournemouth send in a long throw, King gets in a shot and Adrián makes a brilliant save. From the follow-up, Winston Reid makes a fantastic block with his head.

'Don't get your cigar out yet,' I tell Fraser.

'Can we smoke here then?' he asks.

'Yes,' I reply, 'the stewards particularly like you to stand up and smoke...'

Bournemouth's next long throw sees them lose the ball and Mark Noble set Jonathan Calleri clear. He cuts inside the defender well, but then shoots wide when he should make it 2-0.

It's a gritty win in the end, though, and credit to Adrián for making two outstanding saves. Four years after London 2012, history has been made at the Olympic Stadium. Fraser, Michael and I make some more history by persuading Nigel to try a hipster bar at Hackney Wick. Crate has fantastic craft beer, but it's too crowded to get served, so we try the nearby Tank bar set in a suitably distressed old warehouse. Huge metallic tanks of craft beer stand behind the bar. Nigel asks if they do pints. 'That's so last century,' quips CAMRA member Michael as we sip our two-thirds-of-a-pint glasses of Howling Hops ale. Yes, Tank is so hip it is no longer respecting the pint. There's also a deposit that you get back with your glasses, which helps Fraser replenish his wad.

Then it's on to Number 90 on the other side of Hackney Wick station, where the lads drink pints of 'Shithouse' and we sit by the River Lea Navigation and watch the Hoegaarden garden barge moor by the terrace, which is all very different to Upton Park. It starts to rain so we move inside, where loud reggae is playing, flat iron steaks, vegetable terrines and moules-frites are being served and Nigel mutters, 'I never knew so many people went drinking in Hackney Wick…' In the gents we discover there's a man handing out towels. We concur that the person handing out towels in the gents at the Central would have had the worst job in the world.

Three games into the new stadium and I'm starting to quite enjoy it, unless that's just the Howling Hops. We retreat to the Overground as Nigel takes a picture of the derelict traditional pub on the corner, happy with a win and slightly bemused by Hackney Wick's *Sweeney*-esque aura of gentrification. We've got three points at our new home and we might be on trend with our post-match drinking. The *Evening Standard* has a feature headlined, 'West Ham fans descend on hipster haunt Hackney Wick in search for new bars after stadium move', while Yahoo has a video of three West Ham fans leaping into the river near Crate (not advisable, as you may be injured hitting submerged shopping trollies, scaffolding or bottles of discarded beard lotion).

There's one more game at the London Stadium in August: the Thursday night Europa League tie against FC Astra Giurgiu. We're all still learning as fans. Stratford station is struggling to cope with 57,000 supporters at commuter time and there are huge queues by the stairs. We find a new route to the stadium from Stratford Broadway, following a group of fans down the back streets, past a bar in a shed and through a warren of alleyways, railway lines and tunnels that eventually lead to the Orbital sculpture and the stadium. It makes Nigel's legendary short cut from Green Street to the Black Lion seem a model of directness, but the Orbital does look splendid silhouetted against a setting sun.

The game itself is a disappointment. West Ham have nine players out and a weakened side concedes a goal on half-time as Byram and Burke lose the ball and Astra score a breakaway goal. Despite battering the Astra goal in the second half, the Romanians win 1-0 and inflict the first defeat on West Ham at their new home. There's also more argy-bargy with standing fans and the stewards and some incidents between our own fans. Perhaps this is going to be a difficult transitional season.

Part of the problem is that West Ham doesn't control the stadium security. That's down to the E20 partnership, set up by the London Stadium Legacy Corporation and Newham Council. E20 in turn employs the rather Orwellian-sounding stadium operator LS185 (named after Team Great Britain's medal tally at London 2012) to do the stewarding. Some of the old stewards from the Boleyn claim to have been sidelined and it's clear the problem needs to be sorted out quickly. Meanwhile, it emerges that there's no police presence inside the ground because the stadium won't have the correct Airwave radio system installed until December. Perhaps they could use TARDIS-style police boxes instead.

However, amid the frustration is hope. Astra indulge in some terrible time-wasting and rolling around the floor with injuries, which certainly helps to rekindle the noise among the crowd. Fans stand up and holler abuse at a player in white who has stayed on the ground for too long. Howls of frustration pierce the balmy night air. The Anglo-Saxon expletives are not corporate at all and the man in black earns a hearty chorus of 'The referee's a wanker!' Matt has his first tirade of the season at Byram and Burke for losing possession and then at Bilić for bringing on James Collins as an emergency centre-forward. Amid all the anger it's easier to forget that we've moved. Home defeats will feel the same wherever we are.

At the final whistle, Alison behind us remarks, 'It's just like walking into a room full of really angry men…', reprising her 1988 remark made after walking onto the Chicken Run after a long exile in Spain.

'Oh well, it's only a game,' says a fan on the bridge to Stratford.

'But not a very good one,' replies Fraser.

After the match, a twenty-minute walk takes us to the Railway on Leyton Road, which is a good traditional Victorian pub serving Doom Bar that has staff in West Ham T-shirts. We console ourselves by discussing the smallest clubs we've seen West Ham play at, coming up with Macclesfield, Crewe, Shrewsbury and Barnet. We're not going anywhere. What else would we do on a Saturday, Sunday, Friday, Monday, Tuesday, Wednesday, Thursday and whenever else Sky schedule the football?

Online reaction to the new ground remains mixed. Some fans are excited, others incensed by the stalls selling popcorn. My pal Big Joe complains that to get to his seat at the back of the Betway Stand he has to pass a couple of Sherpas and Edmund Hillary. For some fans, the club has become a brand. There are those who say it is soulless and corporate, but then there were probably supporters complaining about the commercialisation of the Claymore whisky advert on top of the stand at the Boleyn in 1904.

Nicola suggests that it's like changing from Doctor Martens shoes to high-leg boots and football fans are always moaning about something. Writing on the Facebook group Upton Parklife, Robert Banks, author of *An Irrational Hatred of Luton*, compares it to the move from primary to secondary school:

> You've been dumped in a place twice the size and you don't know where anything is, you've been split up from your mates, and there's a load of bigger kids, most of whom seem to be standing in front of you. The first few weeks are a bit over-awing. But you find your feet. You find your old mates and make new ones. You find the best bike sheds to have a fag behind. It will all be OK.

We'd all like the ground to be square and for there to be no running track. But it's an iconic stadium, it looks fantastic from the outside and it's enjoyable to be exploring a new area and not have to queue to get inside or to go to the gents. The stewarding will improve. And the lure is trophies. West Ham now have the third largest ground in the Premier League and in theory the increased revenue will help lure world-class players and propel us to the same level as Arsenal, Chelsea, Man City and Man United, becoming by far the greatest team the world has ever seen. In theory, that is.

The big test will come in the games against the likes of Spurs, Chelsea and Man United. It's not going to be Upton Park, but 60,000 fans on a winter's night should generate some decibels. And perhaps we should imagine what it will be like ten years down the line. Then we'll know all the people around us and have established where to eat before the game and where to drink afterwards. A new generation of children will have known nothing but the Olympic Park. We might by then be owned by billionaires who throw so much money at the club and the landlords that they find a way of squaring off the front of the stands. We'll have a history in Stratford and maybe even a cup or two or three or four or more to add to the list on the new stand – well, that or be trying to make the play-offs in the Championship. But my guess is that it's going to be alright, eventually.

A football club is more than a stadium. Those of us who were there will never forget the Boleyn Ground and Harry Redknapp racing down the wing to deliver a cross on an autumnal night. Or Winston Reid rising to score against Man United as de Gea fumbles the ball into the net and the old stadium going 'effing mental. We won't forget the East Stand, Ken's Café, the Boleyn or even the Central. But we can't go back. Change has come and now we have to make it work. So come on you Irons.